Sketches
of
Our Pioneers

To which is added the
Autobiography of Chester Bullard

By
Frederick D. Power

Revised, Expanded and Corrected by
Bradley S. Cobb

Charleston, AR:
COBB PUBLISHING
2024

On the Cover:

Alexander Campbell
Barton W. Stone
Walter Scott
Raccoon John Smith
Thomas Campbell
Samuel Rogers
Moses E. Lard
Jacob Creath, Jr.
Isaac Errett
Elijah Goodwin
Chester Bullard

Thanks to
www.TheRestorationMovement.com
**for permission to use some of the
images on the cover.**

Published in the United States of America by:
Cobb Publishing,
704 E. Main St.
Charleston, AR 72933
CobbPublishing.com
CobbPublishing@gmail.com
479.747.8372

ISBN:

A Note About This Version

Many hours of work were invested in preparing this new version of *Sketches of Our Pioneers*. Typos found in the original have been fixed. Spelling and grammar errors have been corrected. In many instances, long sentences were divided into smaller ones. On occasion, extremely long paragraphs were also divided. Words (such as *he* and *they*) were added frequently when the original was lacking them. In short, the entire book has been meticulously re-edited.

The *Autobiography of Chester Bullard* was not part of the original book, but has been added here (1) to give a fuller description of his life and work, and (2) because it, too, was edited by Frederick Power, the author of *Sketches of Our Pioneers*. It seemed right to include it here. Also included is a short biographical sketch of the author, Mr. Power, which wasn't in the original book. These two additions have also undergone the same extensive editorial treatment as mentioned above.

In addition to these corrections and revisions, the whole book has been reformatted to give you a much more pleasant reading experience.

I hope you enjoy it!

-Bradley S. Cobb,
July 2013

MORE RESTORATION MOVEMENT BOOKS FROM COBB PUBLISHING

Alexander Campbell: A Collection (Volume 2)

Abner Jones: A Collection

The Eternal Kingdom: A History of the Church of Christ

Life of Elder Walter Scott

Memoirs of Elder Thomas Campbell

Life of Raccoon John Smith

Biographical Sketches of Pioneer Preachers of Indiana

Life and Work of R.C. Barrow

Life of Knowles Shaw, Singing Evangelist

Pardee Butler: The Definitive Collection

Autobiography of Barton W. Stone

Rice Haggard: Forgotten Soldier of the Restoration

The Cane Ridge Meetinghouse: Updated Edition

Life of James O'Kelly

Recollections of Men of Faith

Early Relation and Separation of Baptists and Disciples

Origin of the Disciples of Christ

AND MANY MORE!

Available from:
Amazon.com, Apple Books, BarnesAndNoble.com,
BooksAMillion.com, Kobo, and CobbPublishing.com

FOREWORD

From the very first, the reformatory movement of the Disciples of Christ has been honored by the names of men of great faith and "mighty in the Scriptures." Among them were many of marked ability, of excellent learning, and of heroic mold. In their conflicts, with a condition of things inherited from darker centuries, they shattered the traditional dogmatism of many generations. They sought to distinguish between faith and opinion, between the teachings of Christ and his apostles and the teachings which have grown up since New Testament times. As with one voice they plead for freedom from all that is not taught in the Scriptures, either by explicit statement or approved precedent, and for un-compromising loyalty to all that is taught therein. The cardinal points upon which they found themselves in perfect agreement, and for which they earnestly contended with great persistency, have been summarily stated in the following items:

The sufficiency of the Sacred Scriptures as a rule of faith.

That the New Testament contains the will of God concerning *our* duty. In this dispensation of grace, God speaks to us by his Son.

That faith must have Jesus Christ for its object, and not opinions and speculations of men.

That there must be a 'thus saith the Lord,' either in explicit statement or approved precedent, for every article of faith and item of practice.

That sinners must now be told to do just what they were told to do in the days of the apostles to obtain pardon of sins.

That there should be a complete restoration of the ordinances as they were in the beginning.

They protested against sects and sectarianism.

They deplored divisions in the body of Christ, and plead for Christian union.

They demanded, as they gave, the largest liberty in matters of opinion, but asked for unity in matters of faith.

The entire reproduction of the apostolic church, its doctrines in their simplicity, and its practice without change.

In point of time we are getting far removed from the beginning of this religious movement. The present generation is but little familiar with the names and the sacrifices of the heroic men and women who were its pioneers. We owe to them a great debt. We have in them a glorious heritage. We should become acquainted with their characters and their labors and should catch the inspiration of their noble deeds. We cannot too faithfully hold up their teachings and examples as worthy of the admiration of the world and the imitation of our youth.

These sketches are necessarily brief. In a volume so limited we can do but scant justice even to the most prominent figures of our heroic period. Many pioneers will occur to older Disciples that are not even named here. We have aimed to treat, as satisfactorily as possible, the men who were the molders of our policy and directors of our movement in the early time. We lay no claim to originality, but gladly acknowledge our obligation to the different biographers of these pioneers. Leaders of circles should, as far as possible, secure the larger biographies of the men whose work we have sought briefly to outline, and the lives of others not treated in this hand-book. Each circle of readers should make a special study of the pioneers of its own state and should enlist the older church members, who may recall the times of the fathers, to give them the advantage of their personal recollections.

Kentucky must have the lead in this history. Stone is the pioneer of all the pioneers. He and his associates announced to "the church and the world on the 28th of June, 1804, that they took from that day forward and forever, *the Bible alone as a rule of faith and practice to the exclusion of all human creeds, confessions*

*and disciplines, and the name Christian to the exclusion of all
sectarian or denominational designations or names.*" Thomas
Campbell did not come to America until 1807, and the Declaration
and Address" was not published until 1809.

F. D. P.

Washington, D. C., September, 1898.

CONTENTS

CHAPTER I.
BARTON WARREN STONE

This co-laborer of Alexander Campbell was born at Port Tobacco, Md., December 24, 1772. He was the son of John Stone and Mary Warren. When he was very young his father died, and his mother moved to Pittsylvania County, Virginia, in 1779, during the Revolutionary War. General Greene and Lord Cornwallis fought at Guilford Court House, N.C., about thirty miles from his home, and young Stone heard the roar of their guns. He attended school for four or five years, and received instruction in the simpler branches. He was a great reader, but could get but few books. Religion was at a low ebb following the war; the Bible was little read, the Lord's day was given to pleasure, and the houses of worship were deserted. Then came the Baptists into that region, and young Stone was greatly impressed by the scenes he witnessed at their revivals. People claimed to be delivered from sin by dreams, visions, voices or apparitions, or the actual sight of the Savior. "Knowing nothing better," he tells us, "I considered this to be the work of God and the way of salvation." These preachers had a way of affecting their hearers by a "singing voice" in preaching.

Following these came the Methodists, who were very plain and humble, but zealous men, and were warmly opposed by the Baptists, who represented them as "the locusts of the Apocalypse" and warned the people against them. Young Stone's mind was much agitated by their conflicting teachings. He had an earnest desire for religion, and often retired in secret to pray, but, ignorant as to what was required of him, he became discouraged, and joined in the sports of the time.

February, 1790, he entered Guilford Academy, North Carolina, worked hard, lived on milk and vegetables, and allowed himself only six or seven hours out of twenty-four for sleep. There was great religious excitement at the time, and many of the students united with the Presbyterian Church. This was distasteful to him, and he determined to leave the institution, but a little circumstance changed his plans. His room-mate asked him to go with him to hear the preacher. The sermon so impressed him that he resolved to become a Christian. For a year he was tossed on the waves of uncertainty, laboring, praying, and striving to obtain "saving faith," sometimes desponding and almost despairing. The common doctrine was that men were so totally depraved they could not believe, repent, and obey the gospel; regeneration was the immediate work of the Holy Spirit, and *now* was not the accepted time, but the sinner must wait.

While in this state he heard a sermon on the words, "The Sacrifices of God are a broken Spirit." It described his condition, and hope sprang anew in his breast. But another sermon on "Weighed in the Balances and Found Wanting," cast him down as profoundly as before, and his days were full of sighs and groans. Still another discourse, on "God is Love," gave him great comfort, and he found his way to peace.

He was very poor. He could not secure sufficient clothing. But he passed through the Academy, and in 1793 became a candidate for the ministry. The particular subjects assigned him for study were the Trinity and the being and attributes of God. "Witsius on the Trinity" greatly confused him, and before he was licensed he became so unsettled by the doctrines presented that he determined to give up the idea of preaching. Early in 1795 he went to Georgia and became teacher of languages in a Methodist school near Washington. In the spring of 1796, however, he returned to North Carolina, and was licensed to preach. He preached for a time in Wythe County, Virginia, and then journeyed into Tennessee, preaching at Cumberland. The Indians were still in this region, and he had several narrow escapes from them. In 1798 he was regularly ordained pastor of Caneridge and Concord churches, Bourbon County, Kentucky. Knowing he would be required to adopt the Confession of Faith, he determined to examine it. This was the beginning of sorrows. The doctrines of election, reprobation, and predestination, and of the Trinity as set forth in that instrument, he could not accept. When the Presbytery put the question, "How far are you willing to accept the Confession?" he answered, "As far as I see it consistent with the Word of God," and on that statement they ordained him.

His mind was constantly tossed on the waves of speculative theology, the all-engrossing theme of that period. "I believed and taught," he declares, "that mankind were so totally depraved that they could do nothing acceptable to God till his Spirit, by some physical, almighty and mysterious power, had quickened, enlightened, and regenerated the heart, and thus prepared the sinner to believe in Jesus for salvation. Often when addressing listening multitudes on the doctrine of total depravity, their inability to believe, and the necessity of the physical power of God to produce faith; and then persuading the helpless to repent and believe the gospel, my zeal would be chilled by the contradiction. How can they believe? How can they repent? How can they do impossibilities? How can they be guilty in not doing them? Wearied with the works and doctrines of men, I made my Bible my constant companion. I earnestly, honestly, and prayerfully sought for the truth, determined to buy it at the sacrifice of everything else."

In 1801 he was led "out of the labyrinth of Calvinism and error into the rich pastures of gospel liberty." He preached from Mark 16:16 on the universality of the gospel and faith as the condition of salvation, and urged sinners to believe now and be saved. His congregation was greatly affected. He tells how religious excitement ran high at this time. In the revivals scores would fall to the ground pale, trembling, speechless. Some attempted to fly from the scene panic-stricken, but either fell or returned to the crowd, as if unable to get away. An intelligent deist approached him and said, "Mr. Stone, I always thought you an honest man, but now I am convinced you are deceiving the people." "I viewed him with pity, and mildly spoke a few words to him. Immediately he fell as a dead man, and rose no more till he confessed the Saviour."

REVIEW: When and where was B. W. Stone born? Where was his early life spent? What were the religious influences surrounding him? What of his struggles on entering the ministry? To what degree did he accept the confession of faith? How did the doctrine of total depravity affect him? How was he led out of error?

CHAPTER II.
BARTON W. STONE

(Continued)

July 2, 1801, B. W. Stone married Miss Elizabeth Campbell, a pious woman. In August of the same year came the great meeting at Caneridge. "The roads," he tells us, "were crowded with wagons, carriages, horsemen and footmen, moving to the solemn camp." The number was estimated as between twenty and thirty thousand. Methodists and Baptists united with them in these meetings. The services continued six or seven days until provisions gave out. There were many conversions. Most remarkable bodily agitations were seen here. Some with a piercing scream would fall like a log and appear dead for an hour at a time and awake crying for mercy. Others would be seized with "the jerks," sometimes the head alone being affected, jerking backward and forward or from side to side so quickly the features could not be distinguished, or moving backward and forward till the head would almost touch the floor. Wicked people cursing "the jerks" would be seized with this exercise. Sometimes the jerks would cease and they would begin to dance, praying and praising as they moved until they fell exhausted. Barking would also at times accompany this strange affection, and at other times loud, hearty laughter. The subject of these curious agitations would be solemn and his laughter or actions would impress others with the deepest solemnity. It was indescribable. The running exercise was another of these manifestations when, through fear, persons would run until they fell. Some indulged in a peculiar singing, the sound issuing not from the lips but from the breast, and the music was described as heavenly.

Stone was employed day and night, preaching, singing, praying and visiting, until his lungs failed him and he felt that his end was near. His special associates at this time were Richard McNemar, John Thompson, John Dunlavey, Robert Marshall and David Purviance. The distinguishing doctrine they preached was that God loved the world—the whole world—and sent his Son to save men on condition that they believed on him; that the gospel was the means of salvation, but to be effectual must be believed and obeyed by the sinner; that God required men to believe and had given sufficient evidence in his Word to produce faith; that sinners were capable of understanding and believing the testimony and acting upon it by coming to Christ and obeying him, and from him obtaining salvation and the Holy Spirit. They urged the sinner to believe *now* and to receive salvation, that in vain they looked for the Spirit to be given to them while remaining in unbelief. God was willing to save *now*, and no previous qualification was required as necessary to come to Christ.

This teaching aroused the sticklers for orthodoxy, and they cried, "The confession is in danger!" The matter came before the Synod of Kentucky, at Lexington, which resulted in the suspension of Stone and his co-laborers. They were bitterly assailed on all sides. Stone called together his congregations and stated he could no longer conscientiously preach the doctrines of the Presbyterian Church, but would henceforward labor to extend the Redeemer's kingdom irrespective of party, and dissolved his connection with them. At this time, also, he emancipated his slaves and retired to his farm. He continued preaching, however, night and day. He concluded to throw all creeds overboard and to take the name "Christian."

In 1804 he had become disturbed on the question of baptism and was immersed, and came also to feel that baptism was for the remission of sins when Acts 2:38 occurred to him while mourners were gathered at the altar and were being prayed for. But for the full Scriptural views of the design of baptism he acknowledges his indebtedness to Alexander Campbell. In the winter of 1809 his only son died, and in May following his wife died also, leaving four daughters. In 1811 he married again, a cousin of his first wife. About this time A. Campbell visited Kentucky. He saw no distinction between Campbell's teaching and that he had preached for years except on the doctrine of baptism for the remission of sins, and the practice of weekly communion. He did not think Mr. Campbell sufficiently explicit on the influences of the Holy Spirit. In 1831 special meetings were held in Georgetown and Lexington, and a union between the followers of Stone and Campbell was readily secured.

In 1826, Stone began the publication of the *Christian Messenger*. John T. Johnson was associated with him. The work went forward with great success, and A. Campbell's visits to the state gave it renewed impetus. In 1834, Stone moved to Jacksonville, Ill. In 1841 he was stricken with paralysis, still he made preaching tours into Ohio, Indiana and Kentucky. He died at Hannibal, Mo., in 1844.

Some years ago I visited the old Caneridge meeting-house. It was here this great and good man instituted, in the face of great opposition, a church on the Bible alone, and in harmony with Christ the great head of the church. And in pursuance of apostolic example, it was called the "Christian Church" or "Church of Christ." And here on the 28th of June, 1804, he proclaimed to the church and to the world, that he took from that day forward and forever the Bible alone as his rule of faith and practice, to the exclusion of all human creeds, confessions, and disciplines, and the name *Christian* to the exclusion of all, sectarian or denominational names.

The union of Christians on Christ's own terms was nearest and dearest to the heart of Stone. For forty years most sincerely, industriously, consistently, and successfully he advocated this doctrine. He loved the church of God, and wished to see it harmonized. He loved the world lying in wickedness, and longed to see the church united that the world might be converted. Hence when the Campbells came forward to advocate the return to primitive Christianity in faith and practice, laying down the simple terms of Christian union as found in the Scriptures, and sanctioned by common sense, Stone and his co-workers hailed them at once as brethren and fellow laborers in the gospel.

REVIEW: Describe the great Caneridge revival. Who were Stone's co-laborers? What action was taken by the Synod? When were the followers of Stone and Campbell united? What journal did Stone publish and where? What name did his followers accept? What was his aim?

CHAPTER III.
THOMAS CAMPBELL

Thomas, father of Alexander Campbell, was born in County Down, in the north of Ireland, Feb. 1, 1763. He was very devout from his youth. His father belonged to the Church of England and was determined, as he was accustomed to say, "to serve God according to Act of Parliament," but the son was led to prefer the Church of the Secession and early inclined to enter its ministry. He entered the University of Glasgow and completed the literary course of three years, and received his theological training in the Divinity School at Whitburn. June, 1787, he married Jane Corneigle.

After his graduation, Thomas Campbell gave himself to teaching and preaching. In 1798 he accepted the care of a church at Rich Hill, in County Armagh, not far from the town of Newry, within sight of Lough Neagh, and in one of the most beautiful regions of Ireland. Here the youthful days of Alexander were spent. The home was a model Christian home. Father and mother were Bible-reading, praying, godly people. Regular Scriptural instruction and worship were pursued in the household, and

Thomas Campbell sought to introduce the same practice into every home. He was a diligent and faithful pastor. In addition to his ordinary visits, he made a regular tour of his parish twice a year in company with one or more of his elders, inquiring into the state of religion in every home, catechizing the children, examining the older members of the family upon the Bible readings, praying with them, and giving such instructions and admonitions as seemed necessary.

As a preacher he had fine talents and his evident earnestness and personal piety gave great weight to his teachings. The salary of Seceder ministers averaged about $250 a year, and, while the Campbells lived on a farm, they found themselves unable to keep the family on their small income. When Alexander was seventeen, Thomas Campbell opened a school near Rich Hill, associating his son with him in its management. After several years spent in teaching, the excessive labor in discharging the duties of both church and school began to tell seriously upon Thomas Campbell's health. Physicians advised an entire change of life and such relief as a sea voyage might afford. At length it was decided that Alexander should take entire charge of the school and on April 1, 1807, the father started for America, reaching Philadelphia after a sail of thirty-five days. The Anti-Burgher Synod of North America was in session there, received him very cordially, and commended him to the Presbytery of Chartiers in Washington County, Pa., where he again took up the work of the ministry.

The spirit of sectarianism was very bitter in this region. Different branches of the Presbyterian faith would have no fellowship with each other. Mr. Campbell deplored these differences and permitted members of other Presbyterian churches to partake of the Lord's Supper with his people, and was arraigned before the Presbytery for failing to inculcate strict adherence to the church standards. His pleadings in behalf of Christian liberty and fraternity were in vain; they censured him.

He appealed to the Synod and they released him from the censure. Such was the feeling toward him, however, that he finally withdrew from the Synod. He continued to preach in groves and private houses and to plead openly for Christian liberality and union upon the Word of God, and the people thronged to hear him. He found many pious and intelligent Christians who, like himself, were dissatisfied with existing religious parties, the intolerance and sectarianism of the times, and inclined to accept the Bible as their supreme guide. A special meeting was appointed at the house of Abraham Altars, where Thomas Campbell declared his conviction that the sacred Word was all-sufficient and alone sufficient as a basis of union and Christian cooperation. He urged the entire abandonment of everything in religion for which there could not be produced a divine warrant, and announced the sentiment *"**Where the Scriptures speak, we speak; where the Scriptures are silent, we are silent.**"*

"The Christian Association of Washington" was formed Aug. 17, 1809, and the *Declaration and Address* issued September 8, 1809. These marked the beginning of the movement which today enrolls a following of millions. At this time Alexander and the other members of Thomas Campbell's family joined him in the New World. A church was organized on the basis of the principles expressed in the *Declaration and Address* at Brush Run, which in 1811 became a congregation of immersed believers and united with the Redstone Baptist Association.

Thomas Campbell moved to Cambridge, Oh., in 1813 and opened a school. Two years after, he went to Pittsburg and engaged in preaching and teaching. In the fall of 1812 he removed to Newport, Kentucky and for a time taught an academy at Burlington, returning in 1819 to Washington County, Pa. He found but little progress had been made in the work of reform during his absence. The struggle between sectarianism and the principles of the *Declaration and Address* was strong and bitter. His son Alexander was now leading the movement. With the publication of the *Christian Baptist* the principles made great strides. Thomas Campbell made frequent tours, preaching in Western Pennsylvania and the Western Reserve of Ohio, and, while overshadowed in the later development of the cause he pleaded by his more gifted son, his counsels were always potent and his labors untiring and successful.

On the 4th of January, 1854, the long and useful life of this saintly man ended at Bethany. He continued until eighty-three years of age his work of itinerating among the churches. His last sermon was preached in his eighty- ninth year within a few weeks of his death.

"I never knew a man, in all my acquaintance with men," wrote his son, "of whom it could have been said with more assurance that he *'walked with God.'*"

REVIEW: When was Thomas Campbell born and where? What do we know of him as preacher and pastor? What caused his removal to America? Describe the beginnings of our movement. What is said of his later life?

CHAPTER IV.
ALEXANDER CAMPBELL

Near Ballymena, about one mile from Shane's Castle, whose ancient towers are still seen on the northern shore of Lough Neagh, County Antrim, Ireland, Alexander Campbell was born Sept. 12, 1788. His father, Thomas Campbell, was of the Campbells of West Scotland, a minister of the Secession branch of the Presbyterian Church. His mother, Jane Corneigle, was of the French Huguenots. As a boy he was not studious. He tells how on a warm day he stretched himself under the shade of a tree to study his French lesson in Telemachus when he fell asleep and a cow grazing near seized the volume and devoured it, and his father, after sufficiently applying the birch to his person, told him "The cow had got more French in her stomach than he had in his head."

His religious education was not neglected. The synod to which Thomas Campbell belonged prescribed that "The minister should worship God in his family by singing, reading and prayer, morning and evening, catechize and instruct them at least once a week in religion, should remember the Lord's day to keep it holy, and should himself maintain a conversation becoming the gospel."

Religious regimen in the family was exceedingly strict in that day. Reading prayers and catechizing sometimes extended for hours. Of Thomas Campbell it is related that when conducting family worship in his father's house on one occasion, he prayed so long that his venerable parent, rheumatic and irascible, became so distressed by his kneeling posture that he no sooner got upon his feet than in a sudden gust of passion be began, greatly to the surprise and scandal of all present, to belabor poor Thomas with his cane because he had kept him so long on his knees.

Thomas Campbell had great reverence for the Bible. He instilled his views in his son Alexander who, in his seventeenth year, was associated with him in his school and received into membership in the Presbyterian Church over which he presided. In 1807 Thomas Campbell sailed for America and located in Washington County, Pa. In 1808 Alexander with his mother and the younger children took ship to join him in the New World. Off the coast of Scotland they were ship-wrecked, but escaping with their lives, went to Glasgow where Alexander entered the University. Here he came in contact with the Haldanes. These men were reformers who preached a simple gospel. They believed in the independence of the congregations, the Scriptures the only authoritative creed, lay preaching and the toleration of infant baptism. They labored to impress upon men the supreme dignity and glory of Christ. Ultimately, they repudiated the baptism of infants, and, with Alexander Carson, accepted immersion only as Christian baptism.

Alexander Campbell was greatly impressed by these teachings which seemed to him to be more in accord with primitive usage. In August, 1809, he sailed with his father's family for America. When he joined his father he found that providence had guided him into the same liberal and independent views which he had imbibed in Scotland and thus prepared the minds of both father and son for the great work in which they were henceforth to co-operate. Thomas Campbell's fraternity for other Christians, his indifference to ecclesiastical rules, his pleadings in behalf of Christian liberty and brotherhood, and for the Bible as the only standard of faith and life, had brought upon him the censure of his Seceder brethren. He withdrew from them and continued to plead for Christian liberty and union. He had a large following. He did not propose to organize a new church. He dwelt upon the evils resulting from divisions in religious society. He urged that the sacred word was an infallible standard, all-sufficient and alone sufficient as a basis of Christian union and cooperation. He showed that men, not content with its teachings, had gone outside of the Bible to frame for themselves religious theories, opinions, and speculations which were the real occasion of the unhappy controversies and strifes which had so long desolated the religious world. He insisted, therefore, upon a return to the simple teachings of Sacred Scripture and the abandonment of everything in religion for which there was no divine warrant. He set forth in a large meeting of his associates one rule to govern his own conduct and that of all who would accept his principles. "Where the Scriptures speak, we speak; where the Scriptures are silent, we are silent." The formal and actual commencement of the reformation plead by the Campbells began with the declaration of this sentiment. When it was spoken one arose and said: "Mr. Campbell, if we adopt that as a basis, then there is an end of infant baptism." "Of course," was the answer, "if infant baptism be not found in Scripture we can have nothing to do with it." One exclaimed excitedly: "I hope I may never see the day when my heart will renounce that blessed saying of the Scripture, 'Suffer little children to come unto me and forbid them not'." Another said: "In the portion of Scripture you have quoted there is no reference whatever to infant baptism."

These brethren formed themselves into a religious association known as the "Christian Association of Washington," and September 7, 1809, the famous *Declaration and Address* was published. In this Thomas Campbell and those associated with him disclaimed any intention of forming themselves into a church, but associated themselves together for the promotion of Christian union and of a "pure evangelical reformation by the simple preaching of the gospel and the administration of the ordinances in exact conformity to the divine standard." They declared themselves organized for "the sole purpose of promoting simple evangelical Christianity as exhibited on the sacred page, without attempting to inculcate anything of human authority, of private opinion, or invention of men as having any place in the constitution, faith, or worship of the Christian church, or anything as a matter of Christian faith or duty for which there cannot be expressly produced a 'Thus saith the Lord' either in express terms or by approved precedent."

REVIEW: When and where was A. Campbell born? Who were his parents? What was the character of his early religious education? What led to his entrance of Glasgow University? Who were the Haldanes? What had been his father's course in America? What was the formal beginning of the movement? Describe the Declaration and Address.

CHAPTER V.
ALEXANDER CAMPBELL

(*Continued*)

Religious party spirit ran high in those times. Any departure from the tradition of the elders was met with at once with severest ecclesiastical censure. The spirit of sectarianism was rigid and uncompromising beyond anything known to the present generation. Old members were known to break off from their congregations simply because the clerk presumed to give out before singing *two* lines of a Psalm instead of *one* as had been the custom. Against this slavish subjection to opinions and regulations of human origin, Thomas Campbell protested and declared the remedy was to be found in a simple return to the plain teachings of the Bible as alone authoritative and binding upon the conscience.

Such was the state of religious affairs in the community where the Campbells settled when Alexander joined his father. These men little knew what the principles of the *Declaration and Address* involved. A Presbyterian minister referring to the proposition that "nothing should be required as a matter of faith or duty for which there cannot be expressly produced a 'Thus saith the Lord'," said to A. Campbell, "Sir, these words are not sound. If you follow them out you must be a Baptist." "Why," said Mr. Campbell, "is there in Scripture no express precept or precedent for infant baptism?" "Not one, sir," was the reply. Stating the difficulty to his father he merely answered, "We make our appeal to the law and to the testimony. Whatever is not found therein we must of course abandon." Why should we deem it a thing incredible, they reasoned, that the Church of Christ in this highly favored country should resume that original unity, peace, and purity which belong to its constitution and constitute its glory? Is anything necessary for this desirable purpose but to conform to the model and adopt the practice of the primitive church expressly exhibited in the New Testament? Were we in our church constitution and management to exhibit a complete conformity to the apostolic church would we not be in that respect as perfect as Christ intended us to be? Who would not willingly give up his human inventions in worship and cease imposing his private opinions on his brethren and conform to the original pattern laid down in the New Testament that our divisions might be healed? The whole object was to "come firmly and fairly to original ground and take up things just as the apostles left them," and thus "becoming disentangled from the accruing embarrassment of intervening ages" *to stand upon the same ground on which the Church did at the beginning*.

"Never before," says Dr. R. Richardson, "had any reformer taken distinctly such ground as this. Never before had anyone presumed to pass over so lightly the authorities and usages and decisions of so many intervening centuries. Here, indeed, was the startling proposition *to begin anew*—to begin *at the beginning;* to ascend at once to the pure fountain of truth, and to neglect and disregard, as though they had never been, the decrees of Popes, councils, synods, and assemblies, and all the traditions and corruptions of an apostate church. Here was an effort not so much for the reformation of the Church, as was that of Luther and

Calvin, but for its complete *restoration* at once to its pristine purity and perfection. By coming at once to the primitive model and rejecting all human imitations; by submitting implicitly to the Divine authority as plainly expressed in the Scriptures, and by disregarding all the assumptions and dictations of fallible men it was proposed to form a union upon a basis to which no valid objection could be offered. By this summary method, the Church was to be at once released from the controversies of eighteen centuries, and from the conflicting claims of all pretenders to apostolic thrones, and the primitive gospel of salvation was to be disentangled and disembarrassed from all those corruptions and perversions which had heretofore delayed or arrested its progress."

Magnificent conception! Yes, these were magnificent men, men full of faith and of the Holy Spirit, men lifting up in the morning of the nineteenth century the voice of Protestantism which had cried out in the first, "We ought to obey God rather than men!" In a remarkable document covering fifty-four closely printed pages they set forth their principles and purposes. Its spirit throughout is affectionate and Christian though given to the world in an age of bitter religious controversy. Alexander Campbell informed his father that he meant to give his life to the advocacy of these views. In devoting himself to the ministry he declared his firm resolution never to receive compensation for his services. "Upon these principles, my dear son," said the father, "I fear you will have to wear many a ragged coat." The greatness and lofty impulses of this man were never more strikingly manifested than when rejecting all solicitations he received to become the advocate of a party, and the opportunities of distinction which such a course afforded. He determined amidst the contumely and opposition of both the secular and religious world to devote himself to the advocacy of this new movement.

He now gave himself to unremitting preparation for his work. July 15, 1810, he preached his first sermon. Afterwards he spoke constantly in churches, at the cross-roads, in private houses, wherever opportunity offered. The Campbells were still connected with the Presbyterian Church, but the Christian Association was exciting hostility on all sides. In May, 1811, Brush Run Church was organized with 29 members. It was called "The First Church of the Christian Association of Washington County, Pa." Here A. Campbell was ordained to the ministry Jan. 1, 1812.

It was after this that he became greatly disturbed on the question of baptism. Applying himself to the study of the Scriptures and searching critically the signification of the words rendered "baptism" and "baptize," he soon became satisfied they could only mean "immersion" and "immerse." From his further investigations he was led finally to the clear conviction that believers—and believers only—were proper subjects of this ordinance. Sprinkling, he concluded, was wholly unauthorized and that he was, therefore, an unbaptized person. Thomas Campbell had come to the same conclusion. Like A. Judson and Alexander Carson they determined to give up their cherished position and yield to Christ by a solemn burial in baptism. They repaired to Buffalo Creek. Father and son addressed the assembled people, and on a simple confession of faith, with five others, were baptized by Mathias Luse, June 14, 1812.

REVIEW: What is said of the sectarian spirit of the time? What did the "Declaration and Address" involve? How did the Campbells reason? Had any other reformers ever taken this ground? What is meant by Restoration? What was A. Campbell's high resolve? When and where was the first church organized? When and where were the Campbells immersed?

CHAPTER VI.
ALEXANDER CAMPBELL

(*Continued*)

The meeting for baptism when the Campbells were immersed lasted seven hours. Joseph Bryant, one of the members of the Brush Run Church, had to leave to attend a muster of volunteers for the war against Great Britain, and afterwards returned to hear an hour's preaching and witness the baptisms. This was characteristic of the meetings of that day. Men would walk many miles to hear Alexander Campbell and stand for hours listening to him, and the time seemed as so many minutes, so fresh and wonderful were the things he had to tell to the people.

From the moment Thomas Campbell concluded to follow the example of his son in the action of baptism, he conceded to him in effect the guidance of the whole movement. From that hour the position of father and son became reversed. Alexander became the master spirit. This baptism was a decisive step. The necessity felt for unity had brought them to the Bible alone. This led to the simple primitive faith in Christ; this in turn to the primitive baptism in public proof of that faith.

The Brush Run Church was now a church of immersed believers, but in regard to the great principles of religious liberty and progress, as well as the necessity of returning to the faith and practices of the primitive churches, they were far beyond the Baptist communities around them. They had the primitive confession of faith instead of a religious experience, broke bread weekly, and did not observe restricted communion. Immersion seemed the only important difference between the Baptists and other sects. After much solicitation, however, Brush Run Church, with a full statement of their views, united with the Redstone Baptist Association. At a meeting of the Association, August, 1816, A. Campbell preached his celebrated *Sermon on The Law*, which led to his separation from the Baptists.

This was simply a discussion of the relations between the law and the gospel, showing that we are not under Moses, but under Christ, but, it was so much opposed to the theology and style of preaching current among the Baptists of that day, that it caused a sensation.

In the spring of 1820 Mr. Campbell was challenged by Rev. Mr. Walker, a Presbyterian, to a public discussion. The reformers had been opposed to public debates as not favorable to Christian union. The *Declaration and Address* declared "controversy formed no part of the intended plan." Mr. Campbell at first declined to accept the challenge. He was not disputatious, but by repeated urging this was forced upon him. The chief point debated was the identity of the covenants upon which the Jewish and Christian institutions rested. His later discussions, with N.L. Rice on baptism, the Holy Spirit, and human creeds as bonds of union, a debate which lasted sixteen days and over which Henry Clay presided, with Archbishop Purcell on the claims of Roman Catholicism, and with Robert Owen on the evidences of Christianity, are masterpieces of discussion which created a profound impression in their time and did much to extend the principles he advocated.

In 1823 Mr. Campbell began the publication of *The Christian Baptist*. In the first seven years from his little country printing office he issued no less than 46,000 volumes of his works. His writings were read far and wide. His views began to influence large numbers of people. He was assailed as a disorganizer, but it was not his aim merely to overthrow the existing order of religious society. He was well aware of the vast benefit resulting to mankind from Christianity even in its most corrupt forms. He desired simply to dethrone the false that he might re-establish the true, to replace the traditions of men by the teachings of Christ and the apostles; to substitute the New Testament for creeds and human formularies. His work was positive, not negative.

In August, 1823, the second church was organized in Wellsburg, W. Va., with thirty- two members. In October, 1823, A. Campbell visited Washington, Ky., and held a debate with W.L. McCalla, a Presbyterian minister, on the subject, action, and design of baptism. In September, 1824, the Wellsburg Church was received into the Mahoning Baptist Association and Mr. Campbell was a messenger from the church to that body, which met in Trumbull County, Ohio. The same year he made an extensive three months' tour in Kentucky. In 1825 he published in the *Christian Baptist* a series of articles entitled "A Restoration of the Ancient Order of Things," in which he argued the abandonment of everything not in use among the early Christians, such as creeds and confessions, unscriptural words and phrases, theological speculations, etc., and the adoption of everything sanctioned by the primitive practice as the weekly breaking of the loaf, the fellowship, the simple order of worship, and the independence of each church under the care of elders and deacons. This order was then observed in but three churches, Brush Run, Wellsburg, and Pittsburg.

In 1826 Mr. Campbell published "The Sacred Writings of the Apostles and Evangelists of Jesus Christ, Commonly styled the New Testament," with notes. He was thus the first to furnish the English reader a version of the New Testament completely rendered into his own vernacular," as he Anglicized the Greek terms for such words as "baptism" and "baptize." The principles taught by the Campbells were now wide-spread, especially among the Baptists, and in 1827 the Baptist Associations began to declare non-fellowship with the brethren of "The Reformation." From this time we may date the rise of the people known as "Disciples of Christ."

In 1829 Mr. Campbell began to publish the *Millennial Harbinger,* a magazine which he continued to issue monthly until his death. In October of the same year he sat in the Virginia State Constitutional Convention with such men as James Madison, James Monroe, John Marshall, John Randolph of Roanoke, Benjamin Watkins Leigh and others. Ex-president Madison said of him afterwards, "I regard him as the ablest and most original expounder of Scripture I ever heard."

All this time the plea for the restoration of the primitive gospel and original unity of the church went forward. Reformers were increasing in great numbers. Baptist Associations were condemning the errors of Campbell, yet whole churches, and associations even, were taking his position. Indeed Mr. Campbell never intended to withdraw from the Baptist Church. He hoped to carry forward his work among his Baptist brethren. "There never was any sufficient reason," he said, "for a separation between us and the Baptists. We ought to have remained one people and labored together to restore the primitive faith and practice." The Baptists withdrew from him and today hundreds of their churches and tens of thousands of their people hold the principles A. Campbell taught and would receive him in fullest fellowship. He was simply in advance of his times.

In 1839 the great debate with Bishop Purcell was held. In 1840 Bethany College was founded. In 1843 he held his discussion with

N.L. Rice. In 1847 he traveled in Great Britain. This was the busiest period of this great man's life, traveling thousands of miles, speaking constantly, editing, presiding over the college, holding public discussions. His published works number 60 volumes.

In June, 1850, he spoke before both houses of Congress at the Capitol in Washington. His last sermon was on the "Spiritual Blessings in Heavenly Places in Christ." As he neared his end he would look around at those by his bedside and ask, "What think ye of Christ?" and would quote such passages as: "His name shall be called Wonderful, Counsellor, the Mighty God, the Everlasting Father, the Prince of Peace." Lord's Day, March 4, 1866, he passed away.

It is impossible in so short a sketch to describe the life and work of such a man. His influence in history is immeasurable. Think of the little Brush Run Church, just 70 years ago with its 27 members, and now 10,000 churches and 1,100,000 communicants! And this is not the measure. "Surely," said George D. Prentice, "the life of a man thus excellent and gifted is a part of the common treasure of society. In his essential character he belongs to no party, but to the world."

"If I were asked to select a representative of the human race to the inhabitants of the other spheres in our universe," said General Robert E. Lee, "of all men I have ever known, I should select Alexander Campbell; then I know they would have a high impression of what our humanity is like." "There is not a religious body in the United States," said the N. Y. Independent, "whether it would confess it or not, that has not been modified both in spirit and teaching by the influence of Alexander Campbell."

REVIEW: When did A. Campbell take the lead in the work of Reform? Describe the Brush Run Church. What do you know of Mr. Campbell's debates? What journals were published by him? What were his greatest works? Give Madison's estimate of him; Prentice's; Lee's. Describe his end.

CHAPTER VII.
WALTER SCOTT

"Among the helpers and fellow laborers," of Alexander Campbell, "the first place in zeal and ability must be awarded to Walter Scott," says his biographer. "Making the apostles his model, he went before the world with the same message, in the same order, with the same conditions and promises, and inviting instant compliance with its claims." In the little health resort known as Moffatt, in Dumfrieshire, Scotland, sixty-three miles from Edinburg, Walter Scott was born, Oct. 31, 1796. He was of the same ancestry as the great Sir Walter. His parents were John Scott and Mary Jones, strict Presbyterians. He was educated at the University of Edinburg, came to America in 1818, and settled in Pittsburg as a teacher in the following year. He was associated with George Forrester, a Scotchman, who was noted for his piety and love for the Bible. Unlike his brethren in the Presbyterian Church, however, he made the Bible his only authority and guide in religion. Under his influence Scott was not long in making the discovery that infant baptism was without divine warrant; that the baptism enjoined by Christ was a personal and not a relative duty; that it was a matter which could no more admit of a proxy than faith, repentance, or any other act of obedience; and that as he had exercised no volition and obeyed no command when made a subject of the ordinance as taught and practiced by the Presbyterian Church, he had not yielded to his Master's authority in being baptized. He was therefore immersed by Mr. Forrester and united with a small body of baptized believers.

He succeeded Mr. Forrester as principal of the school not long after, but his study of the Bible in the meantime had led him to feel that there was a broader field of service awaiting him in leading thousands as sincere and earnest as himself out of the bondage from which he had been freed. At this time a pamphlet on baptism issued by a small congregation in New York fell into his hands. It so impressed him that he closed his school and went there. He was disappointed, and after three months left New York and visited Baltimore and Washington City, neither of which did he find a congenial field. He continued his travels on foot to Pittsburg and returned to the little flock who received him joyfully. These brethren in their desire to conform to Scripture usage pressed too far some matters which had their origin in the social life of apostolic times. They read the injunction, "Salute one another with a holy kiss," and carried it into practice, becoming known in the community as "Kissing Baptists." The washing of feet they also practiced, not as a church ordinance but as an act of brotherly kindness and hospitality.

In 1821 Mr. Scott's mind became possessed of the great thought of his life, that the central idea of the Christian religion is the Messiahship of Jesus; that the truth that Jesus is the Christ the Son of God is the one fundamental fact of the Scriptures, the creed of Christianity; that this "Golden Oracle" embodied the one true confession for every soul.

January 3, 1823, Walter Scott married Miss Sarah Whitsett. "He was at this time," says one, "about twenty-six years of age, about medium height, slender and rather spare in person and possessed of little muscular strength. His aspect was abstracted, meditative, and sometimes had even an air of sadness. His nose was straight, his lips rather full, but delicately chiseled; his eyes dark and lustrous, full of intelligence and tenderness; and his hair, clustering above his fine, ample forehead, was black as the raven's wing."

It was in this same year A. Campbell projected his first publication. He consulted Mr. Scott, whom he had met two years before, in regard to it. He intended to name it *"The Christian."* Scott suggested that it might disarm prejudice and secure a wider circulation, especially among Baptists, to call it *"The Christian Baptist."* The suggestion was approved, and the periodical which produced the greatest impression on the religious thought of the century was issued August, 1823, under this title. Scott was a frequent contributor, using the pen-name "Philip."

In 1886 Mr. Scott removed from Pittsburg to Steubenville, Oh. In the summer of this year he appeared in the Mahoning Baptist Association as a visiting brother. The following year it met at New Lisbon. Alexander Campbell was one of the messengers, and, going from Wellsburg by way of Steubenville, he prevailed upon Scott to accompany him, and here Scott was chosen "as a suitable person to labor among the churches." This was a surprise, but he proved the man of all others for the place and work, a work which resulted in the dissolution of the Association and the casting off of creeds, and a return to the gospel in its primitive beauty, simplicity, and power.

Religious conditions among the Baptists of this region were, at this time, most discouraging. The churches held to the Philadelphia Confession of Faith. Belief in eternal and personal election to holiness, total depravity, particular redemption, and the irresistible power of the Holy Spirit in conversion prevailed. Reading of church constitutions, covenants, and articles of faith usurped the place of Scripture reading, prayer and praise. Ultra-Calvinism was preached instead of the gospel, and religion languished. Fifteen churches in 1827 reported but 34 baptisms and of these 11 were at

Wellsburg where A. Campbell ministered. In 1825, 17 churches reported 16 baptisms. Great stress was placed upon "the religious experiences" of the convert, his feelings and mental exercises, little accounts taken of change of conduct or personal obedience to commands of gospel. Dreams and visions were tests of conversion. How much of this may be attributed to the reading of John Bunyan instead of John, the Evangelist, we cannot tell. One of the ministers called on to pray for the mourners at a revival exclaimed "O Lord! here are sinners desiring to be converted; Lord they cannot convert themselves; O Lord we cannot convert them. No one, Lord, can convert them but thyself. And now, Lord, why don't you do it?" The preachers taught man's inability to do anything to save himself and the people practiced the doctrine.

Review: How does Walter Scott rank among the reformers? What do we know of his early history? What were the usages of the Pittsburg brethren? What was the great thought of Scott's life. Describe his connection with the Mahoning Association. What is said of the religious conditions of the time?

CHAPTER VIII.
WALTER SCOTT

(Continued)

In 1824 the church at Hiram, Portage County, Ohio, at its monthly meeting determined to renounce its covenant, articles of faith, constitution, and the Philadelphia Confession, and to take the Word of God as the only rule of faith and practice. In the church at New Lisbon, at one of their monthly meetings, the articles of faith were read. One of the brethren asked that the third article be read again; "We believe the Old and New Testaments to be the word of God, and the only infallible rule of faith and practice in religious things." "Brethren," he said, "do we believe that article?" "Certainly, most certainly," was the answer from several. "What then," he demanded, "is the use of the rest if the article just read be true, and the Word of God is the only infallible rule of faith and practice?" The articles were dropped. This was the condition among the churches of the Mahoning Association when Scott began his work as evangelist. The scene of his first practical and successful exhibition of the Gospel as preached in primitive times was at New Lisbon in November, 1827. He showed that the creed of Christianity was expressed in Peter's confession, Matt. 16:16;

that belief of this great truth would produce such love in the human heart as would lead to true obedience; that the great truth of the gospel was first preached on Pentecost in Jerusalem, as Christ had said repentance and remission of sins should be preached in his name among all nations "beginning at Jerusalem;" that Peter preached Christ, and when the heart-pierced multitudes cried under conviction, "Men and brethren, what shall we do?" he gave the reply, "Repent and be baptized, every one of you, in the name of Jesus Christ, for the remission of sins, and ye shall receive the gift of the Holy Spirit;" that the conditions of pardon were unchanged, and as many as gladly receive the word should be baptized and might be at once added to the church, rejoicing in the forgiveness of sins and the gift of God's Spirit.

Many accepted this doctrine. Others opposed and threatened. The whole community began to search the Scriptures like the Bereans of old. The church at New Lisbon almost to a man resolved that henceforth the Word of God should be their only rule and guide.

Scott restored the ordinance of Christian baptism to its proper place as one of the conditions of pardon. Assurance of forgiveness had been made to depend upon the simple exercise of faith. Dreams and visions, unusual sensations and emotions were regarded as tokens of divine favor and proofs of acceptance with God. No fixed and definite way of coming to God and receiving assurance of his favor seemed to be known. Penitents, earnest and sincere, for long periods sought pardon, but their prayers and tears seemed of no avail. John Wesley, for example, under this teaching, was thirteen years seeking God's favor, learning after a long experience of mental suffering "that a sense of forgiveness was his privilege."

Every case of conversion after the gospel was first proclaimed on Pentecost shows that obedience was always followed by the joy of pardon. Scott insisted that all who felt as the multitude who on Pentecost cried out, "Men and brethren, what shall we do?" by obedience to the instructions there given, "Repent and be baptized every one of you in the name of Jesus Christ for the remission of sins, and ye shall receive the gift of the Holy Spirit," might, like them, "gladly receive the Word," and feel the assurance that the promise was fulfilled to the joy of their hearts.

From New Lisbon, Scott went to Warren, and here many were baptized and the whole Baptist church accepted the new order of things with Adamson Bentley, their pastor, who afterward became a tower of strength in the restoration movement.

As illustrating the intense interest in the new views of divine truth thus presented, we have the example of John Tait, a man of strong will and a zealous member of the Presbyterian Church. His wife, under Scott's preaching, resolved to confess Christ and be baptized. He bitterly opposed her and threatened violence to the preacher if he baptized her. She was baptized, however, and soon Tait himself became obedient to this New Testament institution. Not long after he met his former pastor and urged him to be baptized for the remission of sins. "What!" said the minister, "would you have me to be baptized contrary to my conscience?" "Yes," said Tait. "Were you, Mr. Tait, baptized contrary to your conscience?" "Yes," was the reply, "I was. My conscience told me that sprinkling in infancy would do, but the Word of God said, 'Be baptized for the remission of sins,' and I thought it better to tear my conscience than to tear a leaf out of my Bible."

1827-28 was a year of battle and of victory. A great meeting was held at Austintown. John Henry was among the converts as was A.S. Hayden. Deerfield was also the scene of a great awakening. Jonas Hartzell lived here, a most zealous and successful preacher. Indeed it was a current saying through the Western Reserve that all the male members of the Deerfield church were preachers. Everywhere Scott's labors aroused the greatest interest. The new views were canvassed in the field, the forest, the workshop. The Bible was read with new fervor. "The Mahoning became a second Jordan," says Baxter, "and Scott another John, calling the people to repentance." Services were held in barns, groves, dwellings. Baptismal scenes occurred often at night by the blaze of torches or the light of the moon. Nearly every convert became a preacher and every Disciple carried his New Testament, which he used as the Sword of the Spirit. They became known as "Men of the Book," or "Walking Bibles."

Review: What were the conditions among the churches when Scott began his work? What doctrine was proclaimed by him? What element of the Gospel did he restore? What of the work at Austintown and Deerfield? Tell the story of John Tait.

CHAPTER IX.
WALTER SCOTT

(Continued)

Scott arranged the conditions of pardon in their true Scriptural order. Thomas Campbell visiting the scene of his labors in 1828, wrote to his son: "We have long known the theory and have spoken and published many things correctly concerning the ancient gospel, but I must confess that in respect to the direct exhibition and application of it, I am at present for the first time upon the ground where the thing has appeared to be practically exhibited to the proper purpose."

An anecdote of Scott illustrates this arrangement. Riding into a village near the close of the day he spoke to a number of school children and gathered them about him. "Children" he said, "hold up your left hands. Now, beginning with your thumbs, repeat what I say to you: Faith, repentance, baptism, remission of sins, gift of the Holy Spirit—that takes up all your fingers. Now again: Faith, repentance, baptism, remission of sins, gift of the Holy Spirit. Now, again; faster, altogether: Faith, repentance, baptism, remission of sins, gift of the Holy Spirit!" Thus he continued until all could repeat it in concert. The children were greatly amused, thinking him a harmless crazy man. "Children," he then said, "now run home. Don't forget what is on your fingers, and tell your parents that a man will preach the gospel tonight at the school house as you have it on the five fingers of your hands." Away went the children, repeating the story until it was all over the village, and long before the hour of meeting the house was thronged to hear the crazy preacher.

1828-29 Scott associated with him William Hayden, a wonderfully sweet singer and gifted preacher. Great success attended their labors.

At the meeting of the Association at Austintown, over one thousand converts were reported. On this occasion John Henry moved, "that the Mahoning Association as an advisory council or an ecclesiastical tribunal should cease to exist." This marked the formal separation from the Baptists. Up to this time the Association was a Baptist body, though many of their Baptist peculiarities had been abandoned. Those who embraced the new teachings were called "Campbellites" or "Scottites" and after the dissolution of the Association they were known as "Disciples."

The first step of this remarkable man was to fix upon the divinity of Christ as the central and controlling truth of the Christian system. Then he arranged the elements of the gospel in their simple, natural and scriptural order. Next he made baptism the practical acceptance of the gospel on the part of the penitent believer, as well as the pledge or assurance of pardon on the part of its author. Finally, in dissolving the Association he freed the disciples from the last bonds of human authority and placed them under Christ with the Word for their guide.

In 1832 Walter Scott moved to Cincinnati and began the publication of the *Evangelist*. He resided at Carthage, eight miles north of the city for thirteen years. His labors at this period were extremely arduous.

Calls for his services were incessant. His home was a humble one. Once he was the owner of two cows, but a neighbor had none, and soon they were on equality, having one each, and as the gift he thought should be worthy, the neighbor got the best cow. His children complained at this somewhat, not that he had given away the cow, but that he had parted with the one that wore the bell.

His home was a center of gracious hospitality. Fellow laborers like Stone, Pinkerton, Rogers, Jameson, R. Richardson, his former pupil, and others often cheered him with their visits. An incident related by one who visited him at Carthage shows his simplicity of character. "After conversing a few moments he left the room and in a short time returned with a basin of water and a towel, and in the kindest tones said: 'My young brother, permit me to wash your feet,' and he immediately proceeded to do so; and while kneeling at his task kept me engaged in conversation until it was accomplished." Scott gives an instance of this act of hospitality shown him in Baltimore. During the winter of 1841-42 he spent three months in the east visiting Baltimore, Philadelphia and New York. Of his visit to the first of these cities he says: "We repaired to the hospitable domicile of our brother in faith and spirit, Alexander Reed, and certainly never was man by man or brother by brother received in a manner more congenial with the spirit and precept of primitive Christianity than we by him. 'Simon,' said our great and glorious Master to a certain Pharisee, 'I entered into thine house and thou gavest me no water for my feet—thou gavest me no kiss.' Not so with this man of God, this disciple of Christ. He embraced us, kissed us, and graciously washed our feet. Our heart was touched. We thought we saw in the faith and manner of this disciple both the principle and practice of our own dear Redeemer and we made no effort to restrain our tears. We were both silent and we both wept."

In 1836 Walter Scott wrote *The Gospel Restored*, a full and systematic view of the Christian Religion. When on a visit in Missouri he met Moses E. Lard who threw his arms about him and said with much feeling: "Bro. Scott, you are the man who first taught me the gospel." "How so?" Scott asked. "It was by your *Gospel Restored*," answered Lard.

In 1857 he completed his work *The Messiah, or the Great Demonstration*, his effort of greatest literary value. Of this book Dr. R. Richardson declares: "In view of its sublime and far reaching revelations, its cogent logic and still more striking analytical divisions and just distinctions, the rest of the literature of the Reformation seems to me to grow very pale and dim."

In 1840 there was much discussion among the followers of Campbell and Scott as to the name by which they should be known. "Reformed Baptists," "Reformers," "Disciples," "Campbellites," and "Scottites" they were called. In this they wished to be guided by the Word of God. The choice was between "Disciples of Christ" and "Christians." Campbell contended for the former while Scott favored the latter. The name "Disciples" he urged was a common noun and not a proper name at all and argued from Acts 11:26, Acts 26:28, I Pet. 4:16, Rev. 2:13 in favor of the royal name *Christian*.

Walter Scott was a born preacher. He had a rich melodious voice and a face full of expression. "I have heard Bascom and Stockton and many other gifted men, but none to compare with him," says Baxter, "he stands alone." He was a man of rare eloquence but not always equal. In every respect he was a gospel preacher. He went to Christ rather than the Apostles. Twice a week for twenty- two months he discoursed on the gospel of Matthew alone. "If any man would work faith in his audience," he tells us, "let him give his days and nights, and weeks and years to the study of the evangelists." Scott fell asleep in Christ at Mayslick, Ky., April 23, 1861.

Review: How did Scott arrange the Conditions of Pardon? When did the separation from the Baptists take place? What is said of his work in Cincinnati? What of feet washing? Of what books was he the author? Describe him as a man and as a preacher.

CHAPTER X.
JOHN T. JOHNSON

The religious movement of the Campbells was not only thoroughly evangelical, but it was intensely evangelistic. One of the best examples of this spirit among the pioneers is the subject of this sketch. He was born in Scott County, Ky., near Georgetown, October 5, 1788. His parents were Virginians and members of the Baptist Church. Kentucky was then a frontier state and Indians were still committing depredations upon the settlers. He received a fair education, completing his studies in Transylvania University. He studied law and practiced for a time. In 1811 he married Miss Sophia Lewis, a girl of fifteen. In 1813 he served as aid on the staff of Gen. W.H. Harrison and saw active service. After the war he was for several years a member of the Kentucky legislature and in 1820 was elected to congress.

He became a member of the Baptist Church in 1821. Speaking of this he said: "It was a most glorious thing for me. It preserved me from a thousand temptations and kept me a pure man." "During the years '29 and '30," he says, "the public mind was much excited in regard to what was vulgarly called 'Campbellism,' and I resolved to examine it in the light of the Bible. I was won over; my eyes were opened, and I was made perfectly free by the truth, and the debt of gratitude I owe to that man of God, Alexander Campbell, no language can tell."

He began preaching and sought the reformation and enlightenment of the church of which he was a member. As they would not hear him, he, with two others, formed "a congregation of God," February, 1831. He surrendered a lucrative law practice and began his career as an advocate of simple New Testament Christianity. At this time in Kentucky there were eight or ten thousand people variously styled "Marshallites," "Stoneites," "Schismatics," but who claimed to be simply Christians, taking the Word of God as their only rule of faith and practice and repudiating all human creeds. He was soon associated with "that eminent man of God," Barton W. Stone, and became co-editor of his paper, *The Christian Messenger*, then published at George-town, in 1832, the same year the followers of Stone and Campbell effected a union.

"I was among the first of the reformation in co-operation with Stone," he tells us, "to suggest and bring about a union between the Christian churches and that large body of Baptists who had abandoned all human isms in religion." 1833 was a remarkable year in Kentucky. Asiatic cholera swept the state. It was remarkable also for the success of this new plea for the union of Christians and conversion of the world. Thousands were added to the churches. J.T. Johnson was eminently successful. For the first time he extended his labors beyond the borders of the state, visiting Walter Scott at Carthage, Oh., and preaching with great power and acceptance to the people. His advocacy of the principles of reform in the *Messenger* was at the same time forcible and untiring.

In 1834 he closed his connection with the paper, Stone having removed to Illinois, and in the following year he began the publication of the *Gospel Advocate*. In labors he was every way abundant. He preached constantly and gathered into the churches large numbers of converts. In a meeting of ten days in September of this year 135 persons "were immersed for the remission of sins." "There was nothing of excitement peculiar to revivals so called. Nothing was preached to excite the animal feelings. It was the gospel of truth that did the work."

The cause of liberal education had also a large place in this good man's affections. Bacon College, of which Walter Scott was the first president, was founded in 1836 at Georgetown, afterwards was moved to Harrodsburg and later became Kentucky University. Johnson was a fast friend of this institution. His suggestion also that some work should be undertaken for orphan children no doubt had its influence in bringing into existence, through the efforts of Dr. L.L. Pinkerton, that noble beneficence known as The Midway Orphan School.

In the year 1837 he published *The Christian,* in the editing of which he was assisted by Walter Scott. In a meeting conducted by him in Madison County, Kentucky, about this time, 185 persons obeyed the gospel in three weeks. Two meetings held at Caneridge and North Middletown resulted in 300 accessions. A man of most sanguine and buoyant nature, enthusiastic and unwearying in his labors for the spread of the gospel, he was a wonderful evangelist. He never for one moment doubted the correctness of the great principles he advocated and of their ultimate triumph. He was thoroughly absorbed in the work of converting the world and building up a united church as his master passion. He led thousands to decision for Christ. Some idea of the intense interest in the work of these men may be formed from the character of their meetings. They would speak for hours to audiences that never wearied. His labors were by no means confined to his own state. In 1843 he made a visit to Missouri in company with John Smith, preaching at St. Louis, Palmyra, Hannibal, and other points. In 1845 he made an extensive tour in the Southern States, holding meetings in Little Rock, New Orleans, and elsewhere. In 1845 he visited Virginia and labored in Louisa, Caroline and York counties, and in the City of Richmond, meeting with great success.

He was full of the spirit of missions. "The imperious mandate of our King to his apostles," he declares, "is 'Go into all the world and preach the gospel to every creature.' The law says the laborer is worthy of his wages. Can we get along without consultation and co-operation? If we can, there is no need of congregations. Every divine dispensation of God's goodness, Patriarchal, Jewish and Christian, has been distinguished by consultation and co-operation." He suggested an apportionment plan for raising money, that church officers take the list of members and let each member furnish the committee the value of his estate, the committee ascertain at an equal vote what each member has to pay and affix it to his name, and the members be furnished each with a quota in writing." His idea of the relative importance of the different demands upon the benevolence of the church is seen in this illustration: "Let the church decide upon the amount that can be raised without oppression, say $600. Let this sum be divided according to the magnitude of the objects to be accomplished. For example, expend $225 for preaching at home and the support of the poor, $200 for evangelical operations, $100 for colleges, $75 for the education of beneficiaries." Such a system as this, if practiced, he thinks would "soon bear the gospel over America and Europe." He advocated the sending of A. Campbell to England and David S. Burnet to the old world.

He was an ardent temperance advocate. Not only was he a total abstainer, but he publicly opposed the making, vending, and using of intoxicants as "Anti-patriotic, Anti- philanthropic, and Anti-Christian." On this great issue the pioneers were sound. A. Campbell wrote in 1842: "For my own part for more than twenty years I have given my voice against the distillation of ardent spirits at all. I have both thought and said that I knew not how a Christian man could possibly engage in it. And how a Christian man can stand behind the counter, and dose out damnation to his neighbors at the rate of four pence a dose, is a mystery to me, greater than any of the seven mysteries of popery. I wish all the preachers who drink morning bitters and juleps would join the temperance society. All persons too should take the vow of total abstinence who habitually or even statedly or at regular intervals, sip, be it ever so little of the baleful cup."

John T. Johnson fell asleep in Christ on December 18, 1856, at Lexington, Mo., where he was in the midst of a successful protracted meeting. His remains were taken to Lexington, Ky. Thus he fell in the ranks. His whole life for a quarter of a century was a series of protracted meetings. In labors he was as constant as Wesley. A man of delicate frame yet of great endurance and intense enthusiasm, he rested best when most laboriously and successfully engaged in the great work to which he had devoted his life. A man of apostolic zeal and fervor he was an evangelist of evangelists.

Review: Give the early history of J. T. Johnson. What was his peculiar gift? Describe his connection with the work of education. Where was the scene of his labors? Give his financial plan. What was the attitude of the pioneers toward temperance? Give an estimate of his character.

CHAPTER XI.
JOHN SMITH

On the 15th of October, 1784, in Sullivan County, Tenn., John Smith, familiarly known as "Raccoon John Smith," was born, the ninth of thirteen children. That part of the territory of North Carolina was then *The Commonwealth of Franklin.* In 1795 the family moved to Kentucky and settled in Stockton's Valley. The country was thinly settled and John, when twelve years old, was sent by his father one hundred miles on horseback to get seed corn for the planting, his wallet stuffed with bear's meat and wild turkey. Opportunities to acquire an education were wholly wanting. In religious faith his parents were rigid Calvinistic Baptists. When he talked with his father's pastor the good man labored to impress upon him the thought that the sinner is utterly dead so that he could not obey God if he would; and utterly depraved also, so that he would not obey if he could; that he could not please God without faith, nor have faith till it pleased God to give it, and though he might acknowledge it he could never truly feel his desperate wickedness till the Holy Spirit should show him how vile and wretched a thing he was.

He felt that it was his duty to become a Christian, and on the death of his father in 1803, he was led earnestly to seek religion after the manner of the times. In his chamber, in a secret place in the forest, with his face in the dust and with agony in his heart, he wrestled with God, expecting some audible voice, some supernatural vision, that would in a moment assure him of salvation. A spice-wood thicket was his favorite place of prayer. He said to his mother: "I beseech you as my best earthly friend tell me what more I ought to do for I would give the whole world to be a Christian." "Ah! John," she would answer, "you must wait the Lord's time."

As an illustration of the character of the "experiences" related in those days, an ignorant and simple-hearted old man, who was called on to tell what the Lord had done for him, arose and said: "One morning I went out into my woods to pray, and I saw the devil." The people listened, and none more eagerly than Smith who was anxious to learn the Lord's way of dealing with sinners. "I saw the devil," repeated the man. "You may all think it was imagination, but I saw him as plainly as I see the preacher there." "And how did he look?" asked an old brother. "He was about the size of a yearlin'," said the man. "When I saw him I could not pray and so I came home. But I went back next day to the same place and he was gone! Then I was happy for I knew the Lord had saved me out of his hands."

Smith was disgusted with these things. After a long and painful experience, on the 26th of December, 1804, he went before the church and made a simple statement of his religious struggles. "All who believe," said the Moderator, "that the experience just related is a work of grace hold up the right hand." Every hand went up and the next day Smith was baptized and received into the church.

A desire to preach soon took possession of this young disciple and here came another struggle, he must wait for a divine call. It is related of him that in his sleep he was once lifting up his voice so loudly that he awoke his mother, and going to his bedside she cried out: "John, are you distracted, thus to preach without a call?" About this time he received some little instruction in the rudiments of education from a wheelwright who had moved into the neighborhood, and while toiling on the farm, night after night by the light of blazing pine knots he studied the few books that fell into his hands. December 9, 1806, he married, and took his young wife to live in a log cabin, undaubed and without doors or windows, but soon made habitable by his industry. He took part in prayer and song in the religious meetings of his brethren and was urged to enter the ministry, and in May, 1808, was ordained. His zeal was now unrestrained. He traveled from point to point and spoke in groves, cabins, school houses and meeting houses. He had a fine voice and his sermons after the fashion of the times were delivered in a solemn chant. Dwellers among the hills of the Cumberland declared they could sit at their cabin doors and hear him two miles off. He declared the Calvinistic doctrine of the day: "That all men, without exception are dead in sin and can of themselves do nothing to please God; that they are wholly defiled in all their faculties of soul and body; that not only is Adam's guilt imputed to all, but his corrupt nature is conveyed to all; that consequently all are utterly indisposed, disabled, and made op-posite to all good, and wholly inclined to all evil.

"That nevertheless, by God's decree, a definite number of individuals are predestinated or foreordained to eternal life, whom God chose and appointed personally and particularly to glory before the foundation of the world was laid, without any reference to their conduct or character.

"That these elect persons, being spiritually dead and incapable of doing anything good, are, in due time, called and effectually and irresistibly drawn to Christ without any agency of their own, as if co-operating with the Spirit, but are wholly passive; for which elect persons only did Christ die.

"That those who are thus elected, called, and made alive by the Holy Spirit, are enabled by the same divine influence to do many things that are good and right; that they can repent and believe in Christ and understand and obey the Scriptures; but these good works of the renewed man are not in any sense the grounds of his justification or acceptance with God.

"For God decreed from all eternity to justify the elect, although they are not personally justified until the Holy Spirit in due time actually applies Christ to them; that Christ's own obedience to the law is imputed to them as their whole and sole righteousness through faith, which is the work of the Spirit and the gift of God.

"That all who are thus justified can never fall from grace; but will certainly persevere to the end and be saved.

"That all other persons, whether men, women or children, are reprobate—the Holy Spirit giving them neither the disposition nor the ability to do good. They cannot come to Christ, nor did Christ die for them; and therefore, they must perish in their sins.

"Finally, that elect infants, dying in infancy, will be regenerated and cleansed from Adam's sin and Adam's guilt by the Holy Spirit and saved—while non-elect infants will be left to perish in their corruption entailed upon them, and in the guilt imputed to them."

In November, 1814, John Smith removed to Huntsville, Ala. Scarcely was he settled in his cabin before it was burned to the ground and two of his children were lost in the flames. He had been troubled before in preaching the doctrine concerning non-elect infants and his own affliction rendered his perplexity unbearable. As soon as they were comfortably housed in a new cabin the wife sickened and died and he himself was stricken down with the cold plague. After a long illness he grew strong again and at once returned to Kentucky.

The Tate's Creek Association met at Crab Orchard the last of August. Smith attended it. It was hot and the roads were dusty. His horse was jaded and lean, and in a tattered pair of saddle bags swung across his worn saddle he carried a home-spun suit. He reached Crab Orchard covered with the dust of his journey. A pair of home-spun cotton pantaloons, loose enough, but far too short, a shapeless hat, a shirt, coarse, and soiled and devoid of collar, socks too large for his shrunken ankles and hanging down over his foxy shoes made up his curious costume. A great crowd was assembled. He took his seat on the threshold of the meeting house. It was announced that someone would preach to the throng on the outside, and an old friend recognized Smith and asked him to preach. Two young preachers, who looked with contempt on the strange figure sitting on a log near by, arose in turn and attempted to address the people, but failed, and they were dispersing. Finally Smith was persuaded to speak. As he arose his uncouth appearance caused laughter. The people began to go away. His words, however, soon attracted their attention, and the whisper went around: "It is John Smith, from Little South Fork!" "I am John Smith," he said, "from Stockton's Valley. Down there saltpeter caves abound and raccoons make their homes. On the wild frontier we never had good schools, nor many books; consequently, I stand before you today a man without an education. But even in that ill-favored region the Lord in good time found me. He showed me his wondrous grace and called me to preach the everlasting Gospel of his Son!"

"Redemption! Redemption!!" he shouted, and his voice sounded through the woods like the voice of a trumpet. He had been speaking but a short time when a man rushed into the house and going to Jacob Creath, begged him to let all business alone and come at once to the stand. "Why," said Creath, "what's the matter?" "The fellow with the striped coat on that was raised among the coons is up," was the answer. "Come and hear him!"

Creath hurried out. Others followed. The Association broke up. Preachers and people gathered about the platform. Many climbed the trees to listen. When the speaker reached his peroration the multitude arose and stood on their feet, and when he closed every eye was weeping and every heart thanked God for the man without an education. Creath rushed toward him, as he sank exhausted in a chair, and clasped him in his arms. Such was the origin of the name and character of the preaching of this heroic man.

Review: What do we know of the early life of John Smith? What of his religious struggles? Describe the "experiences" of those days. What was the doctrine preached by him? Describe his appearance and sermon at Crab Orchard.

CHAPTER XII.
JOHN SMITH

(Continued)

Christmas Day, 1816, John Smith married Nancy Hurt, and in the following October left Stockton Valley and took charge of four churches in Montgomery county. He continued to read critically the Philadelphia Confession and test its truth by the Inspired Standard. Already he had repudiated the doctrine of infant depravity and reprobation and was weakening on other points in the creed. He soon saw that the doctrine of Personal Election and Reprobation grew out of the dogma that the Holy Spirit must supernaturally convert men to God. This dogma, he saw, rested upon the assumption that the sinner is dead—dead in such a sense that he cannot believe the Gospel, or repent of his sins until the Spirit quickens him into life. And consequently, as all men are not brought to life, the Spirit must pass by some and allow them to perish—not on account of their greater unworthiness, but simply because God in his own good pleasure did not elect them to eternal life. For these Christ could not have died, else he would have died in vain. The entire superstructure of Calvinism he discovered to be based on the notion that moral death destroys man's free agency.

"What is this death?" he inquired anxiously. Christians are said to be dead to sin. Does this take from them the power to sin? May they not, as free agents, still embrace error, and do wrong? If then, the Christian who is dead to sin can nevertheless do wrong; may not the sinner, who is dead to righteousness, nevertheless do right?

He felt the system he had so long preached was but a wind of doctrine without substantial basis. Such was his state of mind when *The Christian Baptist* fell into his hands. He did not dream until now that it was possible for a man to be a Christian, yet belong to no religious party, for he had, as yet, no conception of an undenominational Christianity. In the spring of 1824 he met Mr. Campbell in Flemingsburg, Ky. On entering the town he saw William Vaughn, a Baptist minister.

"Brother John," said he to Smith, "have you seen Brother Campbell yet?" "No, sir," he replied, "I have not; have you?" "Why, I have been with him for eight days and nights, and have heard him every day." "Is he a Calvinist or an Arminian, an Arian or a Trinitarian?" "I do not know," said Vaughn, "he has nothing to do with any of these things." "Tell me, does he know anything at all about heart-felt religion?" "Bless you, he is one of the most pious, godly men that I was ever in company with in all my life." "But do you think he knows anything about a *Christian experience?"* inquired Smith. "Lord bless you: he knows everything," said Vaughn.

Smith was introduced to Mr. Campbell, and as he arose to receive him, *"His nose,"* as Smith used to say, *"seemed to stand a little to the North."* Later, he heard Mr. Campbell preach, and turning to Vaughn after he was through, remarked: "Is it not hard to ride, as I have done, twenty miles just to hear a man preach thirty minutes?" "You are mistaken," said Vaughn, "look at your watch." He looked, and saw that the discourse had been just two and a half hours long. "Did you find out," asked Vaughn, "whether he was a Calvinist or an Arminian?" "No," answered Smith, "I know nothing about the man, but, be he saint or devil, he has thrown more light on that epistle, and on the whole Scriptures, than I have received in all the sermons that I have ever heard before!"

In 1824 John Smith began to preach the great facts of the Gospel and to call on all men to believe them on the testimony of the inspired writers. The New Testament, he argued, contains all that is necessary to be believed or obeyed in order to the enjoyment of pardon and eternal life; and faith comes by hearing the Word of God and is simply confidence in Christ and in all that God has said, promised or threatened in the Scriptures. The Christian Confession is formally contained in the proposition that *Jesus is the Messiah, the Son of God,* the cordial acceptance of which is the faith that, in full dependence on him, works by love and purifies the heart. The penitent believer is introduced into the Church, or Family of God, by a birth of water, or an immersion into the name of Father, Son and Holy Spirit. In October, 1825, a young man, Jacob Coons, came forward in one of his meetings and stated to the church that he had been long concerned on the subject of religion, but had seen no strange sights and heard no strange sounds; that he believed with all his heart that Jesus was the Christ and wished to obey Him.

"Brethren," said Smith, "with the Bible in my hand, if I were to die for it, I do not know what other question to ask him!" Coons was examined no further, but was admitted to baptism on that simple confession; and was perhaps the first exemplification of the ancient order in the State.

The work went forward now with great success; 1828 was a memorable year. Smith was preaching constantly to great multitudes. His comrades went everywhere preaching the Word. One of the measures of reform urged by him was the union of all Christians on the basis of *faith in Jesus as the Messiah and obedience to Him as the only Head of the Church.* Believing that authoritative creeds were divisive in their tendency and contrary to the will of God, he boldly assailed the covenants and confessions of the denominations, and insisted, as the first step toward union, that these should be destroyed, and that in their stead the apostolic Gospel and order must be restored. This ancient Gospel, as it was termed, was simply the tidings that remission of sins and the gift of the Holy Spirit were assured to every penitent believer on submission to the authority of Jesus Christ in the ordinance of baptism.

Six points were presented, Faith, Repentance, Baptism, Remission of Sins, the Gift of the Holy Spirit, and the Resurrection. Facts to be believed, conditions to be obeyed, promises to be enjoyed: *the facts*—the death, burial and resurrection of the Lord Jesus; *the conditions*—faith, repentance, baptism; *the promises*—forgiveness, the gift of the Spirit, eternal life. Faith, destroying the love of sin; repentance, destroying the practice of sin; baptism destroying the state of sin—this was the arrangement. The *Ancient Gospel* was supposed to embrace everything in the doctrine of Christ necessary to make disciples, the *Ancient Order* embraced everything necessary to preserve and perfect them.

Smith usually laid off his discourses, which were from two to three hours in length, in three divisions: In the first, correcting mis-representations; in the second, exposing popular errors, and in the third, presenting the simple Gospel to the people. His labors were incessant. Reviewing the work of a few months in 1828, he said to his wife: "Nancy, I have *baptized* 700 sinners and *capsized* 1500 Baptists." He was traveling and preaching constantly. His patient wife cared for the children and cultivated the farm. Once he stopped at the gate in passing and without dismounting, called to her and said: "Nancy. I have been immersing all the week. Will you take these clothes, and bring me some clean ones right away, for I must hurry on?" and he handed her his saddle bags. "Mr. Smith," she said pleasantly, "is it not time you were having your washing done somewhere else? We have attended to it for you for a long time." "No, Nancy," was his reply, "I am much pleased with your way of doing things, and I don't wish to make any change."

From the time of his renunciation of Calvinism in 1822 to 1828, he received nothing for preaching; when sent out as an evangelist with John Rogers in 1832, his salary was $300. His life was full of stirring scenes and incidents. As an illustration of his kindly humor, and at the same time his remorseless logic, it is related that on one occasion he was holding a meeting on Slate Creek. A Methodist minister nearby was also conducting a revival, and according to the custom of his church, one day applied water to an infant without regard to its struggles and cries. The next day Smith baptized ten persons in a beautiful stream not far away, and seeing the Methodist brother in the crowd, walked up, and seizing him by the arm, pulled him gently but firmly toward the water. "What are you going to do, Mr. Smith?" said the preacher. "What am I going to do? I am going to baptize you, sir!" "But I do not wish to be baptized!" "Do you not believe?" said Smith. "Certainly I do." "Then come along, sir," said the Dipper, as he was called, "believers must be baptized." "But," remonstrated the man, "I'm not willing to go. It certainly would do me no good to be baptized against my will." "Did you not, but yesterday, baptize a helpless babe against its will?" exclaimed Smith. "Did you get its consent first, sir? Come along with me, for you must be baptized!" And he pulled the preacher toward the water's edge; but the man loudly protested and the Dipper released him. "You think, sir," he said, "that it is all right to baptize others by violence, but when you yourself are made the unwilling subject, you say it is wrong and will do no good! Go your way!" "But friends," he exclaimed, turning to the people, "let me know if he ever again baptizes others without their full consent; for you yourselves have heard him declare that such a baptism cannot possibly do any good."

John Smith was one of the leaders who at Georgetown, Ky., on Christmas Day, 1831, and at Lexington, on New Year's Day following, brought about the union between the followers of Stone and Campbell. This he always regarded as the best act of his life.

He was also one of the Board, of which Mr. Clay was president, which governed the Campbell and Rice debate, November, 1843.

In 1865, and again in 1868, he visited Missouri. February, 1868, he preached his last sermon. "What a great failure, after all, would my long and checkered life have been but for this glorious hope of the hereafter!" was one of his last words. He died Feb. 28, and was buried beside his faithful wife, Nancy, sharer of all his labors in the Gospel, at Lexington, Ky., near the last resting place of J.T. Johnson, the evangelist, and Henry Clay, the statesman.

Review: How did John Smith reason himself out of Calvinism? What were his first impressions of A. Campbell? What was the substance of his preaching? Define the ''Ancient Gospel" and the "Ancient Order." How did he argue against infant baptism? What did he regard as the best act of his life?

CHAPTER XIII.
SAMUEL ROGERS

This faithful servant of the primitive Gospel was born in Charlotte County, Virginia, Nov. 6, 1789. His father served through the Revolution and was present at the surrender of Cornwallis at Yorktown. In 1793, the family moved to central Kentucky, and settled in the forest two miles from Winchester, where they lived until September 1801, when they went to Missouri, known at that time as New Spain. They were four weeks on this journey and lived on venison, buffalo meat, and fish, which they found plentiful in their line of travel. The mother carried her Bible sewed up in a feather bed for fear of the priests. "All that I knew of the Christian religion, until I was grown to the stature of a man." says Samuel Rogers, "I learned from those two preachers, my mother and the old family Bible which she took to that country in her feather bed." He had the opportunity of attending school but three months in his life.

In 1809, his father returned to Kentucky, and in 1812 Samuel married Elizabeth Irvin, and soon after, under the preaching of Stone, became a firm believer in Christ, was convicted of sin and immersed. War being declared between England and the United States he volunteered and served throughout the struggle. After the war he entered upon the work of the ministry and preached on both sides of the Ohio River from Portsmouth to Cincinnati. In those days it was the current belief that the Lord called men to the ministry in some extraordinary way, that he opened a door of utterance and put words in the speaker's mouth, and by a special interposition of power he would furnish his outfit, and direct and sustain him on his way. It is not strange with this faith the preacher would start on a tour of several months with only "a cut ninepence" in his pocket.

In 1818, he settled in Clinton county, Oh., where John I. Rogers was born January, 1819. Here he organized the Antioch Church and was ordained by two ministers of the Gospel. "Old Sister Worley" he says, "also laid hands on me, and I have always believed that I received as much spiritual oil from her hands as from the hands of the others." Under the rules of the "New Lights" he could not baptize until this was done. He baptized forty persons at that time and during his ministry over 7,000. Not long after this he made his first preaching tour into Missouri. The country through which he traveled was wild, and often as he camped out in the forest he was awakened by the howl of wild beasts. He saw elk, deer, wolves and bears. He was overtaken by a prairie fire and escaped by firing the grass around him and keeping to the windward of it. He was three months on this tour as an evangelist.

His labors extended now in all directions. He journeyed as far east as Baltimore, where he preached a few discourses and baptized several persons, and held meetings also in Harford County, Md. This trip must have been a trying one for he speaks of his "many privations" and tells how he was forced to sell his Bible and hymn book to pay ferriage and other expenses. On one of these trips he lived for two days and nights on "a few apples," but he tells us "the truth triumphed gloriously." He made a half dozen tours through the State of Missouri, and traveled extensively in

Kentucky, Indiana, Illinois, Ohio, Pennsylvania and Virginia preaching the Gospel to the people and receiving less than his actual expenses. "Both among our preachers and people," he says, "there was prevalent a foolish sense of timidity upon the matter of taking up contributions of money for the ambassador of God. The little that we did receive was collected and given to us in a manner so sly and secret that the giver often appeared more like a felon than God's cheerful giver. When a brother or sister in telling you 'Good-bye,' took hold of your hand in a clumsy sort of a way, with their hand half shut and half opened, you might look out for a quarter or a few cut ninepences. I have had money slipped into my vest and pocket, into my pants' pocket, and in my sack while I was asleep. All this was done that the ministry might not be blamed, and for the purpose of keeping the tell-tale left hand in blissful ignorance of what the right had done."

Rogers first met A. Campbell in 1825 at Wilmington, O. He heard him preach one sermon two hours in length, and afterward had a free and full conversation with him at the home of Jacob Strickle. As he listened to this great teacher, cloud after cloud rolled away from his mind, "letting in upon my soul light, joy, and hope that no tongue can express." He looked upon Mr. Campbell as a modern Ezra sent to restore the lost law of God to the people. "The reformation," he says, "had an easy conquest over all our churches, for the reason that they were right constitutionally; they had taken originally the Bible alone for their rule of faith and practice. This explains the fact of the early triumph of the reformation in the Blue Grass region of Kentucky. Stone, and those laboring with him, had constituted churches throughout central and northern Kentucky upon the Bible and the Bible alone, and all these without exception came early into the reformation. Stone's reformation was the seed bed of the reformation produced by Campbell."

In 1827 Rogers rode 200 miles on horseback to Warren, Oh., to attend the Mahoning Association and to meet with Walter Scott and the Campbells and their co-laborers. He began at once to preach these views with great fidelity and power. "I never *made* a fine sermon in my life," he declared, "but I have preached a great many very fine sermons, yea as powerful sermons as were ever uttered on earth. But all of these fine sermons were borrowed. I borrowed them from Christ and the apostles. They contained the most sublime facts in the universe to be believed, the grandest commands to be obeyed, and the most precious promises to be enjoyed."

November 14, 1833, the day after the great "star-shooting," he started with his family for Indiana. His near neighbors in his new home were Joseph Franklin and wife, who were immersed Methodists. He began at once to preach in a school house and among the converts was Benjamin Franklin, who became a famous preacher of the primitive Gospel. Seven preachers came out of this meeting. His son, John I. Rogers, was one of them. For five years he labored in Indiana. In 1838 he moved back to Ohio, and in 1840 made his third missionary tour on horseback to Missouri. He was the second preacher to carry beyond the Mississippi the doctrine that the Bible and the Bible alone is a sufficient rule of faith and life, Thomas McBride having preceded him.

An idea of his preaching may be gathered from the sketch of a sermon about this time on election, I Pet. 1:1. He showed the election of believers to be according to an arrangement which God had previously made known; that elections in a state are carried on according to the law and the constitution previously arranged and made known, that is, according to the foreknowledge of the framers of the constitution; that every man, elected at all, must be elected according to that previous arrangement made known and promulgated; that the law clearly defined, first, the character of the person to be elected to office, and secondly, the mode and manner of holding said election. God has made and promulgated such a law for the election of men to a place in the kingdom of Christ; that kingdom was set up on Pentecost; Peter was the one chosen to publish the law of election and Jerusalem the place and Pentecost the time, and this one at the proper time and place opened the polls, laid down the rules regulating the election, and 3,000 men were elected according to the previous arrangement of God the Father, etc. He declared the same law in force today and the polls open, and asked all to come forward who desired to be chosen.

On his fifth tour to Missouri he had a most successful visit to Gasconade County. He tells how the primitive teaching was introduced here. A daughter of James Parsons heard him, was convinced of the truth, and demanded baptism at his hands, but her physician prevented her obedience. Later, finding her days were numbered, she desired her father, an unconverted man, to baptize her. He declared himself unworthy to perform the sacred rite. She urged him, saying that the validity of the ordinance did not depend on the administrator. Her family and friends were greatly moved by her dying entreaties. They sent far and near for a preacher, but could find none. Finally, the girl remembered her old colored "mammy" was a pious woman and she called for her and demanded that she should baptize her. The old colored woman consented, a bath tub was provided, and Sarah, the believing girl, was immersed, and rejoiced in the Lord. This opened the doors to the hearts of the people, and the Gospel triumphed in all that region. On this tour he associated with him a young man, Winthrop H. Hopson, who became afterward the gifted and eloquent Dr. Hopson, who did such noble service for Christ.

In 1844 Samuel Rogers settled in Carlisle, Ky., where he remained seven years. He continued to travel and preach constantly and in his eighty-fourth year made his last visit to Missouri. His end was full of peace. "I shall greet," he said, "first of all, my Father, whose hand has led me all the journey through, and my Savior, whose grace has been sufficient for me in every day of trial. And next I shall look around for her whose love and goodness have imposed on me a debt of gratitude to God I can never repay. When we meet shall we not gather up the children and grandchildren and sit down under the shadow of the throne and rest?"

Review: What of the early life of Samuel Rogers? What was meant by a "Call to the Ministry?" What were the views of that time about praying? What does he say of his sermons? Give an outline of one preached by him. What two famous men were associated with him?

CHAPTER XIV.
THE CREATHS

Among the leading preachers who came out from the Elkhorn Association in 1830, and devoted themselves to the establishment of the reformed views in Kentucky was Jacob Creath, Sr. He was born in the Province of Nova Scotia, Feb. 22, 1777. His father and mother, being sympathizers with the Americans in the Revolution, were forced to immigrate to the States, and settled in Granville County, N.C. Jacob became a member of the Baptist Church, February, 1795, and the following June began to preach. He was ordained to the ministry by John Poindexter and William Basket, at the "Roundabout Meeting House," Louisa County, Va., in April, 1798. He became pastor of Kingston congregation, Matthews County, and was a member of the Dover Association with Andrew Broadus and Robert B. Semple. In 1803, he immigrated to Fayette County, Ky., and took charge of the church of which John Gano had been pastor.

A member of the Elkhorn Association when the congregations who preferred God's Word to human tradition were expelled from it, Jacob Creath with John Smith and others who were taunted with the heresy of "Campbellism," was put out without being allowed the privilege of a trial. He at once became a zealous advocate of the new teaching, and brought over whole Baptist churches. By his prudence and mildness he did much to allay the bitter controversies of that period, and with William Morton, John Smith, and others, soon organized a large number of churches of the primitive faith and order. He traveled extensively and baptized large numbers of people.

As a speaker he was gifted with an unusually melodious voice. He was logical, flowery, and pathetic as he wished. He was a natural orator and had great power over an audience. Thomas Campbell said of his defense before the Association, that he had heard "the most distinguished speakers of England, Scotland, and Ireland, but Creath's speech was the most masterly and overwhelming piece of eloquence to which he had ever listened." Henry Clay pronounced him "the finest orator that Kentucky has ever produced." Few preachers were ever so successful in winning souls. In "the great revival" in Kentucky in 1827, he baptized, or aided in baptizing, 1,400 persons. His ministry covered a period of 56 years. March 14, 1854, he finished his course with joy, his last words being "I am happy!"

Jacob Creath, Jr., was born in Mecklenburg County, Va., Jan. 17, 1799. He was one of sixteen children, five of whom became preachers of the Gospel. He was styled Jacob Creath, Jr., to distinguish him from his uncle. At a very early period he began to think of his soul's welfare. In those days people sought Calvary by way of Sinai. "I strove as hard to observe the laws of Moses," he tells us, "as though I had been a Jew. Had I been told to believe on the Lord Jesus Christ, repent and be baptized for the remission of sins, I could have been a Christian at ten years of age, as easily as at seventeen. I never saw the day when I did not desire to be good and please my Maker. I often withdrew to retired places, and prayed to Him that I might see a great light shining around me like Saul of Tarsus, or hear a voice informing me that my sins were pardoned."

April, 1817, under the preaching of James Shelburne, father of Silas Shelburne, he accepted Christ and was baptized. He preached his first sermon in June following. In 1819, he entered the University of North Carolina at Chapel Hill, and in 1821 became a student in Columbia College, Washington, D.C. He located first in Charlotte County, Va., 1823, and then in Kentucky. He attended the Elkhorn Association, 1829, which was assembled at Lexington. There he met with Raccoon John Smith, John T. Johnson, and others whose views he had already adopted. In December, 1829, he accompanied A. Campbell to Nashville. The Elkhorn Association in 1830 excluded him with his uncle Jacob Creath, Sr., and he became at once active in disseminating the principles of reform. He held a notable meeting with John T. Johnson at Versailles in 1835, where 140 confessed with the mouth the Lord Jesus and were baptized for the remission of sins. Great multitudes attended the baptismal service. The roads were crowded with wagons, carts, carriages, footmen and horsemen, pressing forward to witness the sublime spectacle. "Does not the intense interest with which such baptisms are ever regarded," he asks, "indicate that they are the God-originated method of introducing human beings into the kingdom of the Messiah? People do not thus rush from large scopes of country to see a little water poured or sprinkled upon their fellow beings. It was the most delightful meeting I ever attended. I never expect to realize a greater degree of happiness on this side of heaven than I then enjoyed."

He was a very devout man. His habits of devotion were regular and constant. "I have long been in the habit for my own improvement," he says, "of reading the first chapter of Genesis on the first day of every January, and of reaching the last verse in the book of Revelation by the time old Mother Terra had finished her annual round. Acting upon this plan I have read the whole divine book through more than fifty times."

In 1839 he removed to Missouri and began the long and noble service which is gratefully remembered. His ministry was greatly blessed. He planted churches in Hannibal, New London, St. Louis, and many other places. He served also as evangelist, traveling in Illinois, Kentucky, Tennessee, and as far south as Louisiana. In 1849 he ascended the Mississippi as far as St. Paul. "I am the first man," he declares, "that ever preached the primitive Gospel in that new region, as well as the first that ever proclaimed it in Old Virginia."

In 1851 he made a tour through Kentucky, Mississippi and Alabama. He not only traveled widely in the state of Missouri, but every year made long visits in a half dozen other states, preaching constantly, gathering converts, and establishing churches. "Though often weary *in* my work," he says, "I was never weary *of* it. It has been my meat and drink. My manner of passing the time is as follows: In summer I rise at 4 o'clock a. m., and in winter at 5. I next bathe my face, head and feet in cold water. My wife then rises and dresses. I now read a chapter in the Bible. My wife reads in the evening. After reading we unite in prayer. We breakfast between 6 and 7. After breakfast I walk about a mile to a grove of timber, which I have consecrated as an 'oratory.' I then spend fifteen or twenty minutes imploring divine mercy. And I hereby testify to the present and future generations that there, the world shut out, surrounded by the beautiful trees, and flowers and birds, and other useful and innocent creatures that comprehend not the object of my mission among them, I have enjoyed sweeter pleasure in fellowship with Jehovah than this world has ever afforded me."

His labors extended from 1830 to 1872. He saw many experiences of every character. Traveling in Tennessee to a place called "Beech Grove," he passed a camp ground near the early home of James K. Polk, where he met an old negro driving an ox-wagon. Accosting him respectfully, he enquired the way to Beech Grove. Pointing to the camp ground he asked the old colored man what it was.

"Dat, Massa, is de camp ground, Lockridge's camp ground." "What do the people do there, uncle?" asked the preacher. "De white folks, Massa, gets 'ligion dar in August, and dances it away in de winter. Den dey gets 'ligion de same time nex' year and dances it away Christmas and New Years." "What kind of religion do you call that, uncle, that comes and goes with the seasons?" "De 'ligion, Massa, is in de heels!" "What kind of religion have they at Beech Grove?" "Dat is de know-nuffin Campbellite 'ligion." "Where did they get it?" "De white folks brings it from Nashville." The preacher laughed heartily. He had heard of "head religion" and "heart-religion," but this was the first time he had heard of "heel religion."

Review: Who was Jacob Creath, Sr.? What is said of his gifts as a preacher? Describe the early trials of J. Creath, Jr., in finding peace. What were his habits of devotion? Give some account of his labors. What three kinds of religion are mentioned?

CHAPTER XV.
BENTLEY, HENRY, RAINES, HAYDEN.

A group of strong men were gathered about Walter Scott on the Western Reserve, Ohio, to whom we owe much. Adamson Bentley was one of these pioneers. He was born July 4, 1785, in Allegheny County, Pa. His father moved while he was yet young to Trumbull County, Ohio. He confessed Christ and was baptized, and at the age of nineteen he began to preach. With great fidelity he taught Calvinism as the Gospel. He carried this system in his head and the love of God in his heart. At a great yearly meeting in 1837 he said: "I used to take my little children on my knee, and look upon them as they played in harmless innocence about me, and wonder which of them was to be finally and forever lost! It cannot be that God has been so good to me as to elect all my children! No, No! I am myself a miracle of mercy, and it cannot be that God has been kinder to me than to all other parents. Some of these then must be of the non-elect and will be finally banished from God and all good. And now if I only knew which of my children were to dwell in everlasting burnings, oh! how kind and tender would I be to them, knowing that all the comfort they would ever experience would be here in this world! But now I see the Gospel admits all to salvation! Now I can have hope of everyone for eternal happiness! Now I can pray and labor for them in hope!"

In 1810, he settled in Warren, and was ordained and took charge of the church. He was an excellent preacher and a man of great social influence. He was present at the formation of the Mahoning Association, and his ability as a preacher, and tact and dignity as a presiding officer, rendered him one of its prominent members during its entire existence. Tall, manly, graceful, dignified, eloquent and honest, he had great power with the people. He traveled extensively in Kentucky and Pennsylvania, crossed the mountains many times in his saddle, and was constant in labors. When the great principles advocated by Campbell began to make a stir he was one of the first to accept them and boldly seconded Scott when he came to Warren, and the whole church adopted the plan of Union contained in the New Testament. In 1831, he moved to Chagrin Falls. He preached until 80 years of age, and no man in Northeastern Ohio possessed the influence wielded by this princely man.

John Henry was another of this group, perhaps the most brilliant and gifted. His ministry lasted only about thirteen years. He was a native of Allegheny County, Pa. It was said of him that he sung tunes when not a year old though he did not talk until four years of age. He was a skillful musician, playing nine different instruments, and composing music with ease. His religious training had been in the Presbyterian faith. The *Christian Baptist* changed him. He was immersed by Bentley, and in his 31st year gave himself to preaching the Gospel. He was a plain farmer, and among the common people he had great influence. He was full of the divine Word and was called often the "Walking Bible" or the "Bible with a Tongue." Often without any of the studied arts of the orator he moved great assemblies with a mastery that chained attention for two hours at the time. He was tall, six feet and two inches, spare, of sandy complexion and sharp features, quick in his movements and in the operations of his mind, social, kind-hearted, and of a keen and ready wit. Henry's work was felt throughout the Western Reserve. At an early time preaching with A. Campbell near Minerva, many people who had never seen either of the speakers, heard him in the morning and thought it Campbell. After an interval Campbell preached, and many of his hearers said: "We wish that man would sit down and let Campbell get up *for he knows how to preach."* He was a man of One Book. Mr. Campbell said of him: "As a preacher, of a particular order of preachers he had no equal—no superior. He was not only mighty in the Scriptures as a preacher and teacher, but was also eminently exemplary in the social virtues of Christianity." He died May 1, 1844, universally mourned.

Aylette Raines was born near Fredericksburg, Va., in 1797. He was christened in the Episcopal Church at four years much against his wishes. His parents immigrated to Ohio when he was fourteen years of age. He became skeptical from reading Paine's *Age of Reason*, but his mother's pious teachings held him He went to Indiana and engaged in teaching. There he fell in with the Restorationists and adopted their views. "I got religion," he says. "I underwent a great moral change. There was much of the love of God in it. Shrouded as I was in error, yet there were apertures through which the love of God passed through into my heart and made me inexpressibly happy. I now commenced the study of the Scriptures in good earnest and after two years began preaching."

He came in contact with Scott and others preaching the ancient Gospel. Hundreds were being baptized. He concluded to hear Scott for himself. One object he had in view was to bring Scott into debate. In the first sermon he heard, Scott stated what he called "the six points of the Gospel." Greatly amazed and confounded he feared to oppose him lest he should expose himself. The discourse seemed invulnerable. He said, "I can do nothing against the Gospel preached by Scott unless I should live to disgrace it which the Lord forbid."

The next day Raines heard Scott again. His subject was the resurrection. Again he was amazed. Then he heard him on the two covenants and then on the eleventh of Hebrews. Here he surrendered. Scott convinced him that he should lay aside his philosophy and preach the Gospel as the apostles proclaimed it and he began at once to bear his testimony for the truth. When his case came before the Association at Warren in 1828 it was claimed by some that Raines still held his Restorationist opinions, and should not be admitted. Campbell preached on Rom. 14, defining the difference between faith and opinion. It was agreed that if Raines expressed his willingness to preach the Gospel as the apostles preached it, and to retain his opinions as private property, in harmony with the principles of the Reformation there would be no objection. It gave an example of freedom of thought unknown under the creeds and a striking illustration of the liberality of the basis of Christian union advocated by the Reformers.

After the union of the followers of Stone and Campbell, Aylette Raines went to Kentucky and assumed charge of the united churches at Paris where he remained for twenty years and "by his steady unremitting labors and able advocacy of the Reformation principles greatly extended their influence," says Dr. Richardson.

William Hayden is another of this historic group. Born in Westmoreland County, Pa., on the Lord's Day, June 30, 1799, his family removed to the wilds of the new state of Ohio, in 1804, and settled in Youngstown. He struggled with doubt and Calvinism until sixteen and finally fled for refuge to the hope of the Gospel and was baptized May, 1816, uniting with the Baptist Church. In October, 1821, he heard A. Campbell in Warren. "He was then thirty-three years of age," says Hayden, "the sharpest man I ever saw both in appearance and in intellect. His first sermon was from the text 'Thy Kingdom Come.' I soon saw what he meant to make out and I did not intend to believe him, but I could not help believing him." In 1828 he heard Walter Scott, and his direct method of calling sinners to obedience seemed to him rash and dangerous. Hearing Scott again, his first words were, "There is not a man in this house who believes that God means what he says." Then he went on to show that men came to the Bible with their heads full of religious systems and theories and dared not take the Scriptures in any sense inconsistent with these theories less their religious systems be endangered. He vindicated the authority of God's Word as against every system and exalted its sufficiency, truthfulness, and trustworthiness, showing the propriety of relying upon the divine declarations alone, in which the terms of salvation were presented to us for our immediate acceptance.

A complete revolution was wrought in the mind of Hayden. The Bible became to him a new book. The Gospel was a simple development of God's love, and the power of God unto salvation to everyone that believed it. It was no longer a mockery to preach, as someone pretending to offer salvation to all, yet announcing that this was nevertheless reserved for a definite, pre-ordained number known only to God.

Hayden accepted this position and was ordained by Scott and Bentley. His labors from that time were double those of most men, working with his hands as much as other men and yet more in the saddle than most preachers. For twenty-five years he was absent from home 240 days and nights out of 365. He was incessant in preaching, teaching and conversation, public and private; creating openings and occupying them, and when others could be found to occupy them, going forth to break new ground. He, with his brother, A.S. Hayden, projected the Eclectic Institute, now Hiram College, and he had much to do with the origin of the Ohio State Missionary Society. In 1832 he visited New York, and made many tours in New York, Pennsylvania, Virginia, Michigan, Wisconsin, and even Canada. During his ministry of thirty-five years he traveled 90,000 miles, 60,000 on horseback, a distance of twice that of the earth's circumference; preached 9,000 sermons, or 260 a year; and baptized 1,250 persons with his own hands.

He had the gift of song. People would come out to Scott's meetings to hear William Hayden sing. He was full of song and full of songs suited to every condition. Scott said, "Give me my Bible, my head, and William Hayden, and we will go out and convert the world!" He died at Chagrin Falls, April 7, 1863.

Review: Give some account of Adamson Bentley. What do we know of John Henry's work? What great principle was settled in the case of Raines? How was Hayden convinced? What was the extent of his labors?

CHAPTER XVI.
O'KANE, GOODWIN, HOSHOUR, MATHES

Indiana furnishes a most interesting group of Pioneers. John O'Kane, born in Culpepper County, Va., in 1802, was one of the earliest. His ancestors were Irish and belonged to one of the second families of the Old Dominion. At an early age he embraced Christianity and joined the New Lights. About 1830 he left Virginia and located in Warren County, Ohio, where he preached and married. He became a convert to the "Ancient Gospel" and re-moved to Indiana in 1832, locating at Milton, Wayne County. Here he taught school and labored also as an evangelist, traveling and preaching to great multitudes.

In 1833 he went to Indianapolis, preached in a log house on Market Street and attracted great attention. The Legislature then in session tendered him the use of the Court House and crowded to hear him. The preaching was different from anything heard before, so bold, pointed, convincing, buttressed by Scripture, enforced by the commanding voice, expressive eye, and fine oratory of

O'Kane—it seemed to carry everything before it. It was a pentecostal time. A church was organized.

O'Kane made tours in Ohio and Kentucky. Everywhere his labors were very fruitful. He conceived the project of establishing the NorthWestern Christian University, now Butler College. Of a tall and commanding figure, with a powerful voice and great earnestness, and with a ready wit, he added large numbers to the churches. An orthodox preacher refused to debate with him but expressed his willingness to meet Campbell or some leader of the Reformation. Fixing his keen eye on the preacher, and pointing his long finger, after the manner of John Randolph, he exclaimed, "You, you debate with Alexander Campbell? Why if one of his ideas should get into your head it would explode like a bombshell."

Elijah Goodwin was born in Champaign County, Ohio, January 16, 1807, His parents moved to the Hoosier Territory in 1813 and settled near Vincennes. Brought up in the Methodist Church, the Bible and hymn book were his library. In 1819 he came under the influence of the New Lights, made a profession of religion in 1821 and two years later began to preach. On his examination for the ministry he was asked two questions: "What think you of Christ?" and "What do you understand to be the design of the death of Christ?" To the first he answered promptly: "I believe that Jesus Christ is the Son of God," and to the second: "I believe that Christ died to reconcile sinners to God and not God to sinners."

Preachers received little remuneration in those days. Goodwin's coat was out at the elbows and the length of his trousers had evidently been determined on principles of rigid economy. Starting on a journey into Illinois to preach one of his brethren asked how far he was going. "Some 150 miles," was the answer. "How much money have you for the trip?" "Twenty-five cents." The man gave him an additional quarter; he went on his way rejoicing, spent his money for food for his horse, and fasted two whole days.

In 1827, he was appointed regular evangelist by the Indiana Christian Conference. In 1835, he resolved, from his own investigation of Bible teaching on the subject of conversion, to declare the apostle's doctrine as preached on Pentecost. "If I preach the same facts to be believed, and the same commandments to be obeyed; and if people believe and obey, surely all will be well," he reasoned, "for the Lord is faithful that promised." In 1847, he moved to Bloomington, and was associated with J.M. Mathes in publishing *The Christian Record.* In 1849-51 he was pastor at Madison; 1854, he was agent for N.W.C. University; 1856, he became pastor at Indianapolis. He was a constant worker, travelled, edited his paper, engaged in public discussions, and published *The Family Companion.* He answered well, in his life and work, to Cowper's description of "A messenger of grace to guilty men."

Samuel K. Hoshour was a native of York, Pa. As a boy he worked as a farm hand at four dollars a month until 16. It was then decided to put him at the tanning trade, but a trifling incident changed his plans. A school teacher was needed. A miller who had employed him at odd times about his books, said, "Here is Sammy Hoshour, who can write a pretty good hand, can multiply and divide and reduce pints to bushels. Why not try him?" The miller's influence prevailed and he was invested with the birch.

In his 18th year he united with the Lutheran Church; then studied at York and the Theological Institute, New Market, Va., and after serving country churches, was called to Hagerstown, Md., in 1831. His preaching became very Biblical. Luther was lost in the greater brightness of Paul. An unexpected religious interest was awakened in 1834 in the Beaver Creek region near Hagerstown. A preacher appeared in the place who called himself a "Disciple of Christ." He made many converts and established a church. Hoshour was asked to refute his errors and began to study the subject of baptism. On page 2593 of Luther's works he found in a sermon on baptism, preached June, 1520, these words: "In the first place Baptism, in the Greek language, is called *Baptismos*, and in Latin, *Mersio*, that is when a person dips something entirely into the water, the water will cover it; and although in many places it is no more the custom to push the child into the font and dip them, but only to bepour them with the hand out of the font, yet it ought to be, and would be right, that a person should, according to the signification of the word 'taufe,' wholly sink the child or candidate into the water and baptize and draw it out again; as the word 'taufe' comes from ' tiefen,' as when a person *sinks one deep into the water and dips."* He found another Lutheran, Mosheim, p. 108, saying: "The sacrament of baptism was administered in this (the first) century without the public assemblies, in places appointed and prepared, by an immersion of the whole person in the baptismal font."

His next author, Michaelis, one of the most learned of Lutherans, he found, p. 606, to declare: "The external act of baptism is dipping under water. This the Greek word *baptizo* signifies, as everyone acquainted with the Greek language must admit. The baptism of the Jews was performed by immersion; so also was that of John the Baptist. Immersion was practiced till the thirteenth century, and it is desirable that the Latin Church had never allowed a deviation from this. But it did occur, and at the Reformation it was not altered to the primitive form."

As a result of his investigations Hoshour was firmly convinced that immersion in water is the only Christian baptism. He resigned his influential and lucrative position, was immersed, was formally excluded by the Synod, moved to Indiana and taught school and preached. Lew Wallace and O.P. Morton were among his pupils. In 1858 he was chosen president of Northwestern Christian University. He was a man of large usefulness.

None of the Indiana pioneers contributed more to the "Current Reformation" than James M. Mathes. Greatly perplexed by the religious teaching of the time, he resolved to read the New Testament alone. He concluded he must be baptized for the remission of sins, but not a preacher in all the country would baptize him. He had heard of A. Campbell, but regarded him as an arch-heretic; he derived his "Campbellism" directly from the Bible. Finally he talked to an old New Light preacher, who said: "You are right. It is the Lord's plan, and whatever he commands I can cheerfully perform. I am ready to immerse you for the remission of sins."

Young Mathes began at once teaching and preaching. His salary was socks, and country jeans, and farm produce. He taught school and worked with his hands. Great success attended his labors. In 1843 he baptized 607, and in thirty years 6,000. In 1851 he moved to Indianapolis, where he published *The Christian Record*, in all 16 1/2 volumes; also the Works of B.W. Stone, and Letters to Bishop Morris. His work was great and his influence blessed.

Review: Who was O'Kane? What is said of his work in Indianapolis? How did Goodwin answer the questions put to him at his examination for the ministry? Describe his early struggles. How was Hoshour led to change his church relations? What of the pioneer work of Mathes?

CHAPTER XVII.
ALLEN, HOPSON, LARD.

The first Church of Disciples in Missouri was planted by Allen Wright at Antioch, Randolph County, out of which came H.W. Haley, T.P. Haley, Alexander Proctor, and others. T.M. Allen moved to Boone County, Mo. from Kentucky in 1836. He was born in Virginia, October 21, 1797. He was a fine looking man, over six feet, weighing 180 pounds, with a good voice and commanding style; an accomplished, well-educated gentleman. He had a fine estate, and his eminent social qualities and ample fortune gave him access to the best people. He served in the war of 1812, and was trained as a lawyer. B.W. Stone baptized him in 1823 and he was one of the original six members of "Old Union," Fayette County, Ky. Here he was ordained. He planted the churches at Paris and Cynthiana.

After his removal to Missouri he was not only a successful businessman and farmer, but a laborious preacher of the Gospel. He was constantly traveling and holding meetings. In private houses, barns, groves, court houses, in the halls of the legislature, and in nearly all the meeting houses of the state his voice was heard pleading the cause of righteousness and truth, and the union of God's children by returning to apostolic doctrine and practice.

He was a great friend of education. Bethany College owes him much, and Christian College, Canton, Mo., was projected by him together with D.P. Henderson and others. He also led in the establishment of Camden Point Orphan School. His earthly labors closed October 10, 1871.

Moses E. Lard was one of the early workers in the State of Missouri. Born in Bedford County, Tenn., October 29, 1818, his parents immigrated to Missouri when he was fourteen. They were very poor. At seventeen he was not able to write his name and he worked at the tailor's trade for a living. At twenty-three he heard the Disciples and accepted the primitive Gospel, and the next year held his first meeting, the story of which is told in the first volume of Lard's Quarterly.

In March, 1845, he entered Bethany College. He had a wife and two children and under great pecuniary embarrassment made his way through that institution, graduating with distinguished honors. He returned to Missouri and entered actively upon the work of the ministry.

At Liberty and Independence he made his reputation as a writer and preacher. While at the former place in 1857, he wrote his "Review of Jeter on Campbellism." Already recognized as the greatest preacher among the Disciples in Missouri, this book established his reputation as a trenchant and vigorous writer. From Liberty he moved to Camden Point, and for a time was president of the college; then to St. Joseph, where he preached for several years.

In 1859 he made a successful preaching tour in Kentucky, and in 1860 held his debate with Caples. In 1863, he located in Kentucky and began the publication of *Lard's Quarterly*, an able periodical. During the Civil War he made a trip to Canada, and returning became pastor of the Main Street Christian Church, Lexington. He died in 1880.

Mr. Lard was six feet three inches in height, of large and bony frame, small piercing eyes, the mouth of an orator, with strong analytical mind, and wonderful heart power. He often carried his audiences away by bursts of impassioned eloquence. Many incidents are related of his readiness in the pulpit. Preaching once on baptism for the remission of sins a man interrupted him with the question: "Mr. Lard, do you mean to teach that all men who are not baptized will go to hell?" "No, sir, no, sir," replied the preacher instantly, "but I do mean to teach that if you are not baptized you will go to hell, because you know it to be your duty, and if you do not do what you know to be your duty, you will be lost."

On another occasion when preaching on the same subject a man rose and said: "Mr. Lard, if you were on the plains, a thousand miles from water, and a man dying should send for you, and you should convince him of his sins, and he should believe on the Lord Jesus Christ and be willing to confess him, and you knew that in all probability he would die before you could find water to baptize him, what would you do?" Instantly he replied: "Sir, I would start for water, and if the man should die, he would die on his way to obedience."

Dr. Winthrop H. Hopson was another great preacher of this early period. Born in Christian County, Ky., April 26, 1823, of Virginia parents, his family moved to Missouri when he was a child. He was educated in Illinois College, Jacksonville, and while there was an inmate of the home of B.W. Stone. He grew up under the influence of Stone, Allen and Rogers. The latter describes him at 18 as "graceful, gentle and dignified in his bearing, with an intelligent eye and a charming voice; altogether such a one as would at once command respect, and at the same time excite the suspicion that he might be a scion of the stock of F.F.Vs. of old colony times." They preached together. "I did the grubbing, and Winthrop piled the brush, or when Winthrop made the log heaps, I fired them."

During the first seven years of his ministry, Dr. Hopson received $400. In 1848, he graduated in medicine, and in 1851, was appointed State Evangelist of Missouri. He traveled in a buggy for thousands of miles, and everywhere great congregations greeted him and hundreds were converted. From 1852 to 1858 he conducted a successful school at Palmyra, Mo. He was a great student. He never preached a sermon, unless thoroughly prepared, and his sermons were delivered with wonderful power. In 1859 he held a great meeting in Cincinnati which was attended by thousands. He moved to Lexington, Ky., in 1860. From 1864 to 1868 he preached in Virginia, principally as pastor of the old Sycamore Church, Richmond. He returned to Kentucky, and was pastor of the Walnut Street Church, Louisville, and one of the editors of the *Apostolic Times*. In 1874, he became President of Christian University, Canton, Mo. He died in Nashville, Tenn., 1880.

Dr. Hopson was a magnificent specimen of manhood, kingly and martial in his bearing. Waiting one time for a train at a Missouri town, pacing the platform, he overheard two Irishmen talking: "Pat, and can ye tell me who that man is?" "I dunno," said Pat. "Be Jabers," said the first, "I wonder if he thinks he made God Almighty or God Almighty made him!" But there was nothing haughty about this godly man. Gentle, he was, kind, affectionate, and generous to a fault. I knew him well and heard him often. He was a great preacher. To look at him was a sermon.

REVIEW: Who first planted the primitive faith in Missouri? What of T. M. Allen's work? Give the history of M. E. Lard? What anecdotes are related of him? Who was Hopson? Describe him.

CHAPTER XVIII.
BURNET, RICHARDSON, SHEPARD, PENDLETON.

Here is a group of scholars. The movement of the Campbells, like that of Luther and his co-laborers, was marked by its noble culture. The leaders in the sixteenth century were all university men—the plea for restoration has been urged by scholars and thinkers. David S. Burnet was born of Scotch parentage, July 6, 1808, in Dayton, Ohio. When he was eight years of age his father moved to Cincinnati, where he served twelve years as mayor of the city. Educated in the Presbyterian faith while yet a youth, the study of the Bible convinced him his religious position was wrong. He determined to change his church relations, and united with the Baptist Church. He rejected the authority of creeds, declined to accept any test but the divine Word, and based his application for baptism on Romans 10:6-10. Immediately afterward he commenced preaching, though offered an appointment in West Point Military Academy.

Surrounded by influential relatives and friends, and with every promise of wealth and worldly honors, he esteemed the reproach of

Christ greater riches than all the honors of men and became a humble preacher of the Gospel. He began preaching at 16; was called to the pastorate at Dayton at 20; and organized at 27 the Sycamore Street Baptist Church, Cincinnati, out of which grew the Central Christian Church.

March, 1830, he married Miss Mary Gano, daughter of Gen. John S. Gano, and soon after was actively engaged as evangelist in the Eastern States. Especially was he successful in the cities. From 1834-40 he edited *The Christian Preacher*. He also published *The Christian Family Magazine*, *The Christian Age*, and *The Reformer;* edited a Sunday-school Library of 56 volumes, and *The Christian Baptist*. Two years he was president of Bacon College. He served churches in Cincinnati, New York and Baltimore. He was the first pastor among the Disciples and an orator of great power. He died in Baltimore in 1867. "Brethren," he said, "my faith is strong in God. I die in the faith of the Gospel and have no fears," and repeating the 23rd Psalm in English and Hebrew he passed away. At the time of his death he had been chosen president of the American Christian Missionary Society, of which he was formerly Secretary, to succeed Mr. Campbell.

Robert Richardson was a man of vast and varied attainments. Born in Pittsburg, Pa., September 12, 1806, of Irish stock, he was reared in the Episcopal Church and was confirmed by Bishop White in 1824. Leaving the university his family desired him to enter the ministry, but being a very retiring man by nature he shrank from appearing before a public audience and concluded to choose instead, the profession of medicine. Walter Scott had been a tutor in his family and when evangelist on the Western Reserve he called to see the Doctor, then practicing his profession near Pittsburg, and told him he was baptizing for the remission of sins as had been done in the beginning when the Gospel was first preached on Pentecost, as recorded in the second chapter of Acts.

"It seemed to me a very extraordinary proceeding, but, referring to the transactions of the day of Pentecost, I could not deny that the Record sanctioned it. Feeling somewhat unsettled by the discovery that in the beginning converts were baptized for the actual remission of sins, and knowing that Mr. Scott regarded immersion as the action denoted by baptism, I resolved to examine this question particularly, and as I had never before done, having previously confided implicitly in the views and usages of the clergy. I soon fully satisfied myself that the true meaning of the word baptism was immersion; and finding that I had all my life been mistaken and deceived in regard to it, in consequence of trusting to the interpretation of the clergy, I determined that henceforth I would be guided solely by the Scriptures themselves, and that I would follow whithersoever they would lead me."

June, 1829, Dr. Richardson was baptized by Scott. He rode from Pittsburg to Shalersville on the Western Reserve to obey the Gospel. Shortly afterward he removed to Wellsburg, Va., where he resided and gave himself to preaching and practicing his profession. In 1833 he located at Carthage, Ohio. After two years he went to Bethany, W. Va., where for eighteen years he was professor of chemistry in Bethany College and co-editor of the *Harbinger*. He wrote using the names "Discipulus" and "R.R," and his essays on "Regeneration," "The Kingdom of Heaven" and "The Gift of the Holy Spirit" are famous. Dr. Richardson wrote "Memoirs of Alexander Campbell," an invaluable biography and history; "Communings in the Sanctuary," a devotional work of rare value; "Principles and Objects of the Religious Reformation," perhaps the clearest statement yet published of the purposes of Campbell and his co-workers, and "The Office of the Holy Spirit." He was a charming writer and a saintly man.

Silas E. Shepard was born in Utica, N. Y., February 2, 1801. He was a student from his youth. At 16 he became dissatisfied with his baptism as a Congregationalist and united with the Baptist Church. His independent investigation of the Scriptures also led him to lose confidence in human creeds. Having received a thorough classical, medical, and theological course of training he devoted himself to the ministry. After teaching 18 years at Shamokin, Pa., he moved to Canton in 1827. Here he accepted A. Campbell's teaching, a conclusion previously reached by independent thinking. In 1828 he preached at Smithfield. The church resolved "that we pay Elder Shepard for our minister one-half his time, for one year, $150 for his services, payable in wheat at $1 and corn and rye at 50c."

He preached and studied ancient languages until he took a position in the front rank of Biblical scholars. In Greek, Latin and Hebrew he was critical and thorough. He was called to New York and served as pastor of the church on 17th street eight years. He was connected with the American Bible Union as vice-president, member of the board of managers, and translator, and was associated with such men as Conant, Armitage, and others. In 1858 he traveled extensively in Europe and Asia. In 1865 he was connected with N.W. Christian University, and from 1867 to 1870 was president of Hiram College. He was an intimate friend of James A. Garfield. Thousands were brought into the church by Dr. Shepard, principally in the states of New York and Pennsylvania.

One of the ripest scholars connected with the "Current Reformation" is W.K. Pendleton. He is a native of Louisa County, Va., born September 8, 1817. His family, from the earliest history of the Old Dominion, have been honored public servants of the church and state.

When the movement to restore the church as in the beginning first started in Virginia, his father, Col. Edmund Pendleton, and brother, Dr. Madison Pendleton, accepted the plea and founded the celebrated "Gilboa Church," which has been the mother of many of the Virginia churches. His father's house was the home of the Reformation in that region, and in such an atmosphere he was reared. Educated in the best Virginia schools, and in its university both in the classical and law courses, he was eminently fitted for his life work.

When Bethany College was founded in 1841, he was appointed Professor of Natural Philosophy and served the college as professor, vice president and president until 1887. He became co-editor of the *Millennial Harbinger* in 1844, and was for many years its editor, closing the publication in 1870 in its 41st volume. For several years he was Superintendent of Public Instruction for West Virginia. In 1871 the University of Pennsylvania conferred on him the honorary title of Doctor of Laws.

As president of Bethany College, Dr. Pendleton rendered his greatest service. A noble Christian character, a cultured and unblemished gentleman, an accomplished and trained scholar, a logical and gifted teacher of New Testament Christianity, he has impressed himself upon thousands. Honored and beloved he still lives to bless the cause with his ripe counsels and spotless example.

Review: Who were the scholars of the Reformation? Name others. Give some account of Burnet. Who was Dr. Richardson? Name his writings. What important office was filled by Shepard? Give the history of Dr. Pendleton.

CHAPTER XIX.
BULLARD, COLEMAN, SHELBURNE

These sketches would not be complete without some mention of the Virginia pioneers. It was in old Virginia the Campbells first pled for a return to the primitive faith and life. The little "Panhandle" has its most wonderful history from the influences that went out from the "Sage of Bethany." Its country printing press, its school of the prophets, and its great teacher can well claim a mighty share in molding the religious thought and practice of the century. Matthias Luse little knew what he was doing when he baptized those seven persons June 3, 1812. The results of the war of that period between the States and the mother country were trivial compared with the consequences that flowed from that action.

Very early also in Eastern Virginia forces were at work, independent of Mr. Campbell's movement, which looked to the same end. Chester Bullard began urging in the Southwestern part of the State the cause of religious reformation without knowledge of the work in the "Panhandle." His parents were Baptists and his mother a remarkably pious woman. At seventeen he professed conversion at a Methodist meeting, but unable to subscribe to their teaching he remained disconnected from any party. Deeply anxious, however, on the subject of religion, devoted to the Bible, and possessed of an independent mind, he learned that true religion consisted in the knowledge and love of God, and that after faith and repentance baptism was required. His eldest brother about this time, traveling in Pennsylvania, picked up by accident, at a hotel where he was stopping, a copy of *The Christian Baptist*. This he read before going to rest, and was so impressed by it that he advised his brother-in-law, upon his return to Montgomery County, Va., to subscribe for it, saying the editor was a half century ahead of his age. This was done. During the same year, 1831, Dr. Bullard completed his medical studies and began the practice of medicine in Giles County. Earnestly desiring baptism, he was unable to obtain it at the hands of the Baptists, unless he united with them, which he did not wish to do. He made known his views to Landon Duncan, a minister of the Christian Connexion, who baptized him and he at once began to preach, delivering his first discourse the same evening.

Dr. Bullard presented simple views of the Gospel, declared its salvation to be freely offered to every creature, and showed that faith came by hearing and he that believed and was baptized should be saved. He organized his first church near the source of the Catawba in 1833. By degrees most of those in connection with Duncan gave in their adhesion and a number of churches were organized in that part of Virginia. These people were called "Bullardites." The doctor used to tell of an old German brother who in his public prayers besought the Lord to open the eyes of the Methodists "dot dey might all come over and jine Bullard!"

In 1839, Dr. Bullard happened to take up and read Campbell's "Extra on Remission" at the house of his brother-in-law. Up to this time he had held the strongest prejudices against Campbell. Surprised and delighted with the new views this extra gave of the

Gospel he immediately sought out all the numbers of the Harbinger, and was overjoyed to find how clear and consistent were Mr. Campbell's views and how different from the slanderous misrepresentations circulated through the press and pulpit. He immediately began to circulate these writings, preaching with great success the reformatory principles, and happy in finding himself associated with a host of fellow laborers in the same cause. Hearing Mr. Campbell was to visit Charlottesville he determined to meet him and ever afterward kept up with him constant Christian fellowship.

Dr. Bullard travelled all over Virginia preaching, baptized thousands, and organized a great number of churches. He was an earnest man, a strong preacher, an exhorter of great force, and an untiring worker. He lived to a ripe old age, honored and loved by all.

Reuben Lindsay Coleman was born May 13, 1807, near Scottsville, Va. He was of Baptist parents. The death of his mother when he was nine years of age profoundly impressed him and led to serious religious reflection and great prayerfulness. The death of his eldest brother when he was sixteen deepened these impressions and he resolved to become a Christian. He attended the meetings of the Methodist Church and sought at the mourner's bench the benefit of their prayers but failed to find peace. He gave himself to Bible study and prayer. Such were his anxieties that his health gave way. Finally he became satisfied that Christ was the Son of God, that he came to save sinners, and was both able and willing to save them, and he felt also that he was a sinner and would give the world to become a Christian. He asked, "Why am I not saved? Christ needs not to be made willing by the intercession of preachers for 'He that is willing to come unto me, I will in no wise cast out.' I love God and the people of God. I pray to God and desire to serve him, yet have no assurance that my sins are forgiven." He determined to offer himself for baptism. The Baptists received him as a fit subject, and he was no sooner buried with Christ than he arose from the water with new views and feelings. His faith, perfected by obedience, had become effective, the darkness of his mind passed from him, he realized that his sins had been washed away by the blood of Christ, and, that of this he had received, in baptism, the assurance he had so long sought in vain.

Mr. Coleman at this time knew nothing of A. Campbell's teachings. From what he had heard he regarded him as a semi-infidel. Soon after his baptism he began preaching and held a meeting in Charlottesville, where he organized a church, and in May, 1831, was ordained as its pastor. He was very popular and in labors was abundant and successful.

For the first time, during the Constitutional convention in 1830, he heard Mr. Campbell in Richmond at the First Baptist Church in a discourse of three hours on the Covenants. Embracing these views he became one of the most zealous and eloquent of Mr. Campbell's co-workers, accompanied him in many of his tours, and labored with great success. Mr. Campbell held him in special regard. In the *Harbinger* of 1845 he says: "His eloquence is truly evangelical. It is the eloquence of good sense, of refined sentiment, of deep feeling, and of impassioned earnestness. He has been so much in communion with apostles and prophets, so long and so intimately conversant with their writings, as to have caught their spirit and acquired their solemn and impressive manner of presenting the will of God and its sovereign claims upon the affections and the acquiescence of all his hearers."

No better description of Mr. Coleman could be written. He reminded his hearers of one of the old prophets. An ungodly man said he would go farther to hear Lindsay Coleman say "O Lord!" than to listen to any other preacher that ever lived! On one of Mr. Campbell's visits to Philadelphia he announced that Mr. Coleman had arrived and would speak alternately with him during the evenings of the week. He spoke accordingly the next evening, but having a very modest estimate of himself, and feeling that the people would desire to hear Mr. Campbell; he took the cars for home, and left Mr. C. as he said, "to alternate with himself."

Mr. Coleman edited, with J.W. Goss, *The Christian Publisher* in Charlottesville. He died in Florida, April 21, 1880.

Silas Shelburne was the "Raccoon" John Smith of Virginia. He was born, June 4, 1790, the son of James Shelburne, a Baptist minister. After deep religious convictions he was baptized, June, 1816, and soon after was ordained to the ministry. He was very successful from the beginning. He was remarkable for his good common sense, strong character, poetic spirit and oratory. While aiding his father in a protracted meeting, several persons having professed conversion, presented themselves for membership. His father said, "Let them be examined to see whether they can give a satisfactory Christian experience or not." "Father," said young Silas, "that is not in accord with the teaching of the apostles. How can these men who have been sinners all their lives, and who have never lived a Christian life, give a Christian experience? They can only give a sinner's experience. You might as well require every young couple who come to you to be married, to give a married experience before you perform the marriage ceremony." "Go on, Silas, and do right," said the old man. They were received on their Confession of Faith in Christ. Reading *The Christian Baptist,* he was impressed with the "ancient order of things" and introduced it in the churches. Violent opposition soon arose against these efforts to change Baptist usages and theories and the churches for which Shelburne labored separated from the Meherrin Association.

He traveled extensively in the state and by his faithful preaching and pure life did much to extend the principles of reform. He was a member of the historic conference in Richmond called to consider the matter of Union between the Baptists and Disciples. There were sixteen representatives from each church. Among the Baptists were Jeter, Poindexter, Burrows and Broadus, and among the Disciples Pendleton, Goss, Henley, Ainslie, Walthal, Crenshaw, Duval and Hopson. It was at this meeting

Father Shelburne said to Dr. Jeter when he wished to hear the Baptist articles read: "Trot out yer calf, Jeremiah. When I goes to buy a calf I always wants to see him before I buys him. Trot out your calf!"

Numerous anecdotes of this character are told of this quaint, guileless, yet powerful and fearless preacher of the heroic age. At a preachers' meeting where the brethren were under criticism someone gently suggested that Brother Shelburne might be more useful as a preacher if he would avoid certain peculiarities of speech as "agin'" for against, and "gwine" for going, etc. The old man arose and said: "Brethren, if that is all you got agin' me, I'm gwine 'long." A preacher noted for a certain indefiniteness in his sermons preached before him on one occasion and asked his opinion of the discourse. "Wall, brother," said the old man, "thar's a pint down here on the bay they call 'Pint No Pint.' You were as near thar today as you'll ever be." Someone asked him at a meeting where he preached in the presence of Mr. Campbell if he was not afraid to preach before Alexander Campbell. "No," he replied, "I have preached before Almighty God many a time, and I don't know why I should fear to preach before Alexander Campbell!" Present one day at a baptizing in Old Sycamore Church, Richmond, as the pastor, W.J. Pettigrew, withdrew to the dressing room, and a dead silence prevailed, he arose from the front seat where he had stretched himself, and turning his beaming face upon the congregation, said: "Brethren, sing a song while Brother Pettigrew has gone to change his breeches!" There was a sensation as they raised the hymn:

"How happy are they who their Savior obey."

He died Sept. 7, 1871. Three of his children and three grandchildren have been preachers of the Gospel.

REVIEW: What is said of the position of Virginia in this history? Who was Chester Bullard? How did he become associated with Campbell? What is said of the struggles of Coleman? Give some account of Shelburne.

CHAPTER XX.
ISAAC ERRETT

Of the generation immediately following the pioneers, the most conspicuous figure is Isaac Errett. If anyone after Campbell could be said to have taken the position of leader among the Disciples it was the editor of the *Christian Standard*. Isaac Errett was born in the city of New York, January 2, 1820. His father, Henry Errett, was from Arklow, South Ireland. His mother was Sophia Kemmisli of New York. They had seven children of whom Isaac was the fifth. Henry Errett was himself a man of talent and piety, and published, at twenty-three years of age, a work on "The Constitution of the Apostolic Churches."

When Isaac was five years of age his father died. He was sent to school and never forgot his first teacher—an Englishman whose h's were always in the way, and spelled and pronounced the word "hell"—"haitch-he-double-hell, 'ell" In 1832 the family removed to Pittsburg, and the following year Isaac was baptized in the Allegheny river by Robert McLaren. His mother secured a place for him as boy of all work in a book store. He resolved to become a printer and in his seventeenth year bound himself to Mr. A.A. Anderson, in whose office he became a master workman. "During my apprenticeship," he tells us, "I diligently employed my leisure hours in studying, and having but limited means to rely on, kept bachelor's hall and lived on about one dollar per week that I might have means of improvement." He gives at this time two rules of his life:

"1. I will, with the help of God, rise at four o'clock and spend until six in reading the Bible and prayer.

"2. Monday and Tuesday shall be devoted to the *Intelligencer*, Wednesday to general reading, Thursday to the study of some science until noon, the remainder to visiting, etc., Friday and Saturday to preparing for the service of the Lord's day."

In 1839 and 1840 he was engaged in school teaching. He gave much time to the church and spoke often in the public services. April 21, 1839, he preached his first regular sermon and June 18, 1840, was set apart as an evangelist. His salary was $300. His work in Pittsburg was successful, his fame as a preacher spread abroad, and in 1840 he was called to New Lisbon, Ohio. This was the first church to come out fully upon the ground held by the Disciples seventeen years before. New Lisbon agreed to pay Mr. Errett $500 a year. The first year they raised $250; the second year they arranged for $250 for half his time; the third year he was compelled to raise all his salary by holding meetings. His work of five years here was richly blessed. March, 1849, he removed to North Bloomfield. While here he took great interest in the founding of the "Western Reserve Eclectic Institute," now Hiram College. He was constantly in demand as an evangelist. On one occasion, preaching near Bloomfield, only one person was present at his appointment. The preacher, nothing daunted by the smallness of his audience, read a chapter, sang a hymn, prayed, sang another hymn, and then preached and extended an invitation. The congregation arose and responded with one accord. He said it was the only instance in his experience in which *the whole congregation came forward!* This auditor was Edwin Wakefield who became one of the most successful preachers among the Disciples.

In 1850 Mr. Errett divided his time with Warren. The same year he made an extensive tour in New York. His pastorate at Warren extended over a period of six years, and in the spring of 1856 he removed to Michigan, where he labored principally at Muir, Ionia, and Detroit, from 1856 to 1865. In 1857 he was chosen corresponding secretary of the American Christian Missionary Society, and also served for a time as co-editor of the *Harbinger*, and agent of Bethany College.

Mr. Errett was called to the Biblical department of Hiram College in 1865, and December 22 of that year the first meeting was held at the home of T.W. Phillips, Newcastle, Pa., out of which grew the Christian Publishing Association and the *Christian Standard*. James A. Garfield, W.S. Streator, J.P. Robinson, T.W. and C.M. Phillips, G.W.N. Yost, and W.J. Ford were chosen directors, and Isaac Errett editor. There was a general demand for a weekly paper which should exhibit the apostolic spirit as well as the apostolic letter, and this the projectors of the new journal aimed to supply. It was first issued from 99 Bank Street, Cleveland, April 7, 1866, and its first page was devoted to a memorial of A. Campbell who had just fallen asleep.

The object of the paper as set forth by the editor was three-fold: (1) The turning of the world to Christ. (2) The union of believers in the fellowship of the Gospel. (3) The education of Christians into a nobler spiritual life. "It is the only weekly among us," he said later, "that advocates organized effort for missionary purposes." In July, 1869, the paper was removed to Cincinnati.

It was now that Isaac Errett began his great work. The influence of his voice and pen in directing the movement inaugurated by the pioneers cannot be overestimated. The grand principles for which they had contended were luminously stated and ably advocated by him; the cause saved from a narrow, selfish, and sectarian spirit that threatened its life; and the great and vital interests of unity, organization, and aggressive spiritual and evangelistic power were preserved and mightily enlarged. He was easily the man for the time.

In November, 1871, Mr. Errett held a week's meeting in Augusta, Georgia, for which the church gave him a freewill offering of $ 1, 000. The same year he preached regularly for the church in Chicago, and continued at intervals to do so till 1875. His earnest advocacy of organized missionary work among the women of the church had much to do with the organization of the C.W.B.M. in 1874; and under his leadership also, the Foreign Christian Missionary Society came into being in 1875, of which he was made president. His labors at this period were immense. Preaching constantly, lecturing before the colleges, editing his paper, directing the missionary interests, conducting an enormous correspondence, burdened with the care of all the churches—he was worked to the utmost limit. His faithfulness even in the minute details of business may be inferred from his remark to the writer of this sketch that not a line entered the *Standard* which did not pass three times under his eye.

In 1880 Mr. Errett prepared his "Evenings with the Bible," pronounced "the crowning literary work of his life," and issued in three volumes. His other works given to the public at different times were "Our Position," "Walks About Jerusalem," "Talks to Bereans," " Letters to Young Christians," "Life of Geo. E. Flower," and "Linsey Woolsey and Other Addresses." His writings, in the noblest Anglo-Saxon, are characterized by great clearness, vigor, logical arrangement, profound insight, chaste and delicate humor, thorough and satisfactory treatment. He was one of the most symmetrical of men, well balanced, full-orbed, grandly adjusted. Physically, intellectually, spiritually, he was great. His influence cannot die. December 19, 1888, he joined the hosts about the Throne.

Review: Who is most prominent among the leaders of the generation following the pioneers? Give the history of Errett's youth. What were the rules of his life? What is said of his work at New Lisbon? Tell of the founding of the *Standard* and its object. What of Mr. Errett's connection with the Missionary Cause? Of his writings? Of his character and work?

The Autobiography of Chester Bullard

Edited by Frederick D. Power

Originally appeared in the *Christian Standard*, 1893

On Monday, February 27, this veteran preacher of the gospel entered into his rest. His name is a household word among Virginia Disciples and his fame has reached the furthest bounds of our brotherhood. He is the last of the pioneers for the cause of primitive Christianity in the Old Dominion, and was a man of such forceful character, extended service, varied gifts, noble prominence and long identification with the movement for the restoration of New Testament order and the union of God's people, that he deserves to be held in grateful remembrance. The facts of his life deserve to be more widely noticed than those of ordinary men. It chanced to be my good fortune to know him from my boyhood, and four years before his departure for the better land he has been so long seeking, he placed in my hands an autobiographical sketch to be used in the *Christian Standard* after he had left us. It now becomes my sad duty to comply with his wishes, and I give the interesting story in his own words.

-Frederick D. Power

Part One

Framingham is the name appropriated by a township in Massachusetts, surrounded in early times by Indians, the converts of the Apostolic Elliot, fourteen miles south of Concord and twenty-one miles west of Boston. Bullard is a name frequently occurring in its records, most frequently in its church history. Seth Bullard, born one hundred and eighty years ago, was regularly employed to prepare the record of the religious experience of those who were seeking communion in the Congregational church. He was a praying man, repairing daily to his chaise-house for secret devotion. One Sunday morning while engaged in family worship his wife discovered cattle in the corn lot, and motioned to her grandson, Daniel—my father, then a child—to drive them out. He went out and whistled for his dog. When he returned to the house his grandfather reproved him for whistling on the Lord's day, and to his apology replied: "Could you not have called, 'Here, Bolus!'"

His son Ebenezer, my grandfather, was equally pious, but not so scrupulous about whistling on the Lord's day. The religious tendency in the Bullards was not diminished by their intermarriage with such families as Rice, Stone, Haven, Cook, Beeches, Freeland, Fisk, etc., nor did it lessen the large percentage of those who gave themselves to the ministry of the gospel. This appears from the earliest period to have been the favored family calling. Omitting the names belonging to the seventeenth and eighteenth centuries, and all excepting my own family in the nineteenth, I had two brothers who were preachers. My father not infrequently occupied the pulpit. My next older brother was an elder in the church, and two nephews and my only son are preachers. A social meeting never wanted a tongue to voice their devotions when my mother or one of my two sisters was there. One of my earliest recollections is kneeling beside my mother at the bedside and hearing a voice which time cannot silence. When five years old, while gathering berries with other children, I thought we had sinned, and I proposed to pray, which I did, with feelings of deep contrition.

Notwithstanding the earnest efforts to make me a Christian, a terrible mistake was made in not showing me the Father-side of God. In my childhood, I loved my father, and especially my mother, more than God. I feared God. I remember one night, when probably four years of age, lying on my back, and looking up at the light fleecy clouds which were covering over the disk of the moon, and being almost in an ecstasy until I remembered that God was there, and then I jumped up in a fright and ran into the house. At the same time I thought that everything that was kind, was comprehended in the Christian. A horse in the neighborhood— which had won the sobriquet of "church-horse," because of its connection with a church squabble, I had invested with every enviable quality—not distinguishing between the terms church and Christian—and accordingly I made a swing of the horse's tail while hitched at my father's gate, and to my father who rushed to rescue me, I explained that a Christian horse would not hurt anybody.

At nine years of age I was removed to Staunton, Virginia, and there I attended a school of a pious Methodist class-leader, who habitually prayed in his school. This was calculated to increase my religious anxiety. I uniformly on Saturdays visited Judge Browne's, to secure the supply of butter for my sister's table. Beside the path a little white oak was embowered with a grape vine, a beautiful retreat for prayer, where week by week with alternations of hope and despair, I struggled to secure the forgiveness of sins and the assurance of pardon. It was after my removal to Montgomery county, in my seventeenth year, that I became almost hopeless of ever being numbered with the redeemed. I determined to make one supreme effort and then accept my fate. My sister, Mrs. Snow, became acquainted with my miserable condition, and induced me to consent to invite some religious persons to talk and pray with me. I knelt by my chair, and for hours persevered in the struggle for peace, every effort being succeeded by increasing despondency, just as a convict condemned to death with every failure in attempting to secure reprieve feels the rope tightening around his neck. At last sensibility gave way. My extremities grew cold, the blood retreating to the heart and larger arteries. I ceased to pray and almost to feel I was lifted into my seat. My sister, overwhelmed with anxiety, gazed most earnestly into my face and said, "There is a change in Chester!" There had indeed been a change, for until that word was spoken I was almost insensible; but as I had almost unbounded confidence in my sister Mary, I gathered hope from that sentence. The mental condition reacted upon the physical; there was an instant reaction in the circulating medium, the blood rushed to the extremities, making my toes and fingers tingle, which I accepted as the operation of the Holy Spirit.

There was, in reality, no change in character. There has been, in fact, no time from early childhood when I would not have gladly laid down my life for the assurance of an interest in Christ, and my fear of not securing it made me often wish I had never been born, or that I had been born an imbecile or had died in infancy.

However, if there be any virtue in error here, then was an instance of it, for the serenity which had resulted from the struggle enabled me with a well-balanced mind to search the word of God. I very soon learned that God had no disposition to perpetuate a quarrel with one of his offending creatures, but that he only wanted the prodigal to come home. My friends thought that I ought to unite with some religious body. The Methodist was the only one within my reach. There I found lovely spirits to whom I became fondly attached. But in reading my Testament I found the Christ died to reconcile the world unto God, while the Methodists taught that he died to reconcile God unto the world. I believed that we were justified by faith working by love and purifying the heart which led to obedience; the Methodists, that we are justified by faith alone. I made no concealment of my views, and the preacher in charge told me I was not a Methodist, and advised me to procure a discipline. This only made the matter worse. Hence, one of the sorest trials of my life was a separation from a people I so dearly loved and who had truly loved me, but now turned their backs upon me. And I was led to believe there was not a being on earth that sympathized with me. Even the Great Commission was not understood by others as I read it. With me it was an invitation to salvation on the condition of a loving trust In Christ and a baptism unto Christ.

I now went in search of someone to immerse me; someone who venerated and practiced the ordinance. A Baptist preacher told me I could only receive immersion by first being received by the Baptist church, but I could neither find Baptist church nor its conditions of discipleship in the New Testament. One view that I entertained at this time, so offensive to the religious tastes of the day, was my estimate of the object of preaching which was to reconcile men to God, to be effected by such an exhibition of Christ as to make God understood and loved. And the time came when I felt it my duty to forego all the hopes of early manhood in the effort to reconcile the people of God. This implied an abandonment of every expectation of worldly success and the channels through which happiness had been anticipated. I had exhausted my means in preparing to practice medicine. Like most young men, I had not escaped the fascinations of the other sex, and was in reality engaged to an almost life-long loved one. Could I be so cruel as to expose to ostracism one so universally loved, to bring down upon her head an odium inseparable from the career I had marked out for myself? I laid the whole case before her and yet, woman-like, though sorely disappointed, she refused to renounce me, and I scarcely know a standard by which to measure her devotion during her short life—a life that was a necessity in that crucial period of my career.

No one at this day can understand how "He that believes and is baptized shall be saved," or pardoned, sounded fifty or sixty years ago. A Christian body without a creed was, they said, in the elegant metaphor of the time, a tub without a bottom. And that the faith that saved a soul came through the word received through the ears on the outside of the head was almost a sin against the Holy Ghost. Saving faith came immediately to the heart.

Up to this time, 1836, when I had planted six churches, I was ignorant of having trenched so much upon "Campbellism," a heresy so terrible in my estimation, for a preacher had told me that Campbell taught that a mental acceptance of Christ as the Son of God and an immersion in water made the subject as pure as an angel. At first I was heard by very few persons. My first convert was my wife. Talking with her on the subject of conversions, the influence of a knowledge of God's goodness and its power to win the heart, God's plan burst upon her mind and she was extremely happy and anxious to be baptized.

But how did I receive my baptism? Just below the New River, White Sulphur Springs, rises the majestic cliff, the summit of which is known as Thomas' Hill. There Joseph Thomas, the White

Pilgrim, spent a portion of his early life. He was one of the most laborious and enterprising preachers in the early years of the nineteenth century. Landon Duncan, originally a Baptist preacher, became very much widened by intimate association with him. Duncan was of good report. While he was filling the office of assessor, he spent a night at the New River White, where I made his acquaintance and demanded baptism at his hands, which he finally decided to administer with the understanding that I should preach my convictions, though somewhat divergent from his own and those of Barton W. Stone, with whom he affiliated; and on the 11th day of December, 1830, I was baptized in Sinking Creek at the house of Parker Lucas, and that night preached my first sermon. My views were pretty generally received by the associates of Duncan and Lucas. Subsequently Duncan and Lucas were almost sick of their bargain, but their members very generally sustained me. Ultimately the most amicable relations were sustained between Brother Duncan and myself, and his son Elisha, a preacher, while Parker Lucas antagonized me to the last, though nothing occurred between us that caused me to distrust his fidelity to conscience, or that disturbed our mutual esteem, and all of his family gave in their adhesion, and his grandson, C.S. Lucas, became a powerful proclaimer of the gospel, much of whose ability, in my judgment, was latent in his grandfather.

Now the question arises, how did the brethren in Southwest Virginia become willing to exchange the name "Bullardite," with which their enemies had stigmatized them, for one which had been with them even more distasteful? Thus it occurred. In a journey from the East, through the western part of Pennsylvania, my eldest brother, at a public house where he was stopping, picked up one of the last numbers of the *Christian Baptist,* which he perused before retiring. On returning to his family in Montgomery County, he recommended his sister, Mrs. Snow, to subscribe to the periodical, asserting that its author was half a century in advance of the age. Two numbers of the *Baptist* were received, succeeded by two volumes of the Millennial Harbinger, and would have been read had my sister lived. She dying, they were packed away on a shelf until they were covered with dust. All at once it occurred to me to let A. Campbell speak for himself. The first utterance I laid hold of was from his Extra on Regeneration. Up to this time I had not noticed Acts 2:38, and the charge of the disciples to begin at Jerusalem. Believe me. I was not long in getting to Jerusalem, where the whole road into the kingdom of heaven was illuminated with a brightness exceeding that of the electric light of our day; where the process of the regeneration was illuminated with three thousand examples.

When David Crockett first became the proprietor of a Johnson-Walker dictionary, he declared his readiness to spell against Adams and his whole cabinet. Now I felt ready to spell against all the contrivances for getting religion. Up to this time I had been enabled, from various passages, especially the Commission, to lead thousands to Christ and a good conscience. No one reared under the present administration of the Word, where "the beginning at Jerusalem" is not ignored, can know what "the beginning at Jerusalem" was worth to me. In Giles County, where I was baptized, God's great, loving heart was more fully understood, and the way in which Christians may become a unit without sacrifice of conscience, was, for the first time, clearly understood by them, while Parker Lucas' views of a unanimity of religious sentiment as necessary to union were abandoned. A meeting house was built, and many added to the church. At Gravel Hill, fifteen miles above in the same valley of Sinking Creek, a church, already strong, was greatly enlarged, and a good house was built, greatly through the instrumentality of one of its charter members, Jacob McPherson. This is the only man who told me, after I had preached on the beginning at Jerusalem, that he had often asked the preachers to preach as Peter did. This man reminded me of my great grandfather in his extreme conscientiousness. He was in the habit of resorting to Gap Mountain to spend the day in fasting and prayer. Bright and early one morning, as he started out, he was reminded of the passage, "Anoint thy head and wash thy face." He thought, *how can I anoint my head without oil*. He remembered that his wife had churned the day before, and the spring house being in his path, he proceeded to butter his head, and surely there was water enough to wash his face, for I have baptized scores in that beautiful stream. And he washed his face and went on his way. Since that he has shaken his sides laughing at the illustration of the way in which a literal obedience may contravene the divine purpose.

Part Two

There is one incident in my never-to-be-forgotten intercourse with Jacob McPherson that I will relate, as it is a singular one. He was a most God-like man, one of the most efficient Christians—probably *the* most efficient—in the county in which he lived. On one occasion I had been preaching at Gravel Hill, but without fruit. Bro. McPherson was there early for nine o'clock prayer-meeting. I met him in the yard, and he said to me with animated countenance: "There will be accessions today." I observed, "I see no hope." "Never mind," he replied. I preached and I believe twelve came forward. I exhorted and still asked for confessions. I was about to dismiss the congregation when he came to me and said: "Stop, Bro. Bullard, till I count!" and he proceeded, and, getting through, remarked there was one lacking. I then told the congregation that Bro. McPherson believed there was another in the audience who would carry away a sore heart if a disobedient one, and a gentleman some fifty years of age from the most remote seat arose and came forward, and the count was up. Jacob McPherson's dream was accomplished.

Gravel Hill is midway between Sugar Grove and New Castle, the county-seat of Craig County, where I suppose I have baptized five hundred persons, nearly all of whom are in the other world. I wish to name several of the preachers in this field, especially those early in the work. Claiborne Curtis, starting from Mecklenburg

County to the West, had the misfortune to break his leg, and was for a long time confined in the vicinity of New Castle. He was a Baptist, a school teacher, with gifts as a public speaker. He heard me frequently, and was glad to see me receive the confession of his wife and baptize her. He became an elder in the church at New Castle. He afterwards removed to Raleigh County, West Virginia, where he and his wife were the only members in the region in which he lived, and thinking the gospel perverted by what he heard, determined himself to try to preach it. There was a young man in the county who had, when a little boy, heard me preach in Peterstown, Monroe County, and was willing then to make confession, but thought I would not receive it on account of his extreme youth. He now came forward, and Bro. Curtis baptized him. His name was Carper. The two, as long as Bro. Curtis lived, were pillars and supports of a spreading church, and Carper still lives.

D.A. Snow was baptized when fifteen years of age. James Calfee when probably nineteen. Both have made their mark, commencing to preach when they were young men. Snow, my nephew, was for some time pastor of the church in Jackson, Mississippi, and is widely and favorably known. The county of Mercer is more indebted to Calfee than to anyone dead or alive. He has passed to his reward, not only for work done there, but at various points of useful service.

The church at Cypress Grove received an early and valuable accession in the person of James Redpath, a local Methodist preacher. He was left in charge of the Salem Methodist Church, but despite everything he could do, one after another of his people were buried with Christ in baptism. He first determined to forbid any preaching in the Salem house of worship, but then I preached under the oaks, and he was said to be hid in the Chinquapin bushes. I was again admitted to the house. Either way there were the same results. The preacher in charge of the circuit consulted with him as to what was to be done. Redpath advised that "the chickens still left should be taken away and put under the old hen at Bethel," "For," said he, "by the time you get around again Bullard will have the old rooster!" He was immersed and his last was the most useful years of his life.

Within five miles of my home resided Hezekiah Whitt of the Baptist Church. It was not hard for him to do what he saw to be his duty. He united his labors with mine, choosing as the text of his first sermon: "If they hear not Moses and the prophets neither would they be persuaded though one rose from the dead." It was so easy to follow him with the indubitable evidence that faith comes by the Word of God that I never failed to make him preach from the same text when asked on what subject he should preach. No one finally was more willing to accept God's plan of salvation than Hezekiah Whitt, and he urged others as long as he was able to preach. His wife, who could never accept Baptist teachings, and his children accepted the gospel as the power of God unto salvation.

Having learned from some tobacco traders passing through the country that John T. Wooton, of Prince Edward County, who had been discipled by Jacob Creath, on becoming a citizen of Henry County, had discipled two brethren in that county, I determined to visit that section. A very successful meeting not only established a strong church at Horse Pasture, but one which dominated the public sentiment of the region. Subsequent visits planted the cause in the lower end of the county at Mt. Vernon; also at County Line; later Pittsylvania Court House, now Chatham. By this time incidental visits from Silas and Cephas Shelburne and the permanent labors of Dr. Hugart established the cause in Southern Piedmont.

I finally responded to a call to one of the border counties of North Carolina. Among my hearers was a young skeptical lawyer and his bride. Retiring from the church he observed: "This is putting the case in an entirely new light. I must re-examine it." A few months later he alighted at my door, spent a few days with me, and returned a preacher of the gospel of the grace of God, winning souls to Christ. His name was Virgil A. Wilson.

Other States are indebted to Southwest Virginia—Kentucky, Missouri, Washington, etc. Preaching in West Virginia, Powhatan Baber, one of my hearers and a Baptist, after listening to a single sermon on God's plan for the union of Christians, was thoroughly convinced and made the best time I have ever seen in a church from the seat he occupied to give in his adhesion. His efficient labors are divided between the two States. The same may be said of Bro. Lineburg, of Carroll County. He was a Baptist preacher who, with his church, joyfully united with us on the one foundation laid in Zion. Afterward he removed to the West—dead or alive, he is one of the Lord's noblemen.

A very valuable accession was made from the Presbyterian church—Thomas G. Shelor, my brother-in-law, who was welcomed in every congregation and strong in the faith, though he fought every step of the way from Presbyterianism and his wife from Methodism to a burial with Christ in baptism, and thought, I believe, for some time that he was going to capture me, always preparing during my absence to retrieve a defeat.

While returning a visit of Coleman and Goss to Piedmont, I was induced to pass through Southeast Virginia, and preached at Mt. Olivet, Lunenburgh County. Shortly after my return home two men from that county came to my house to induce me, if possible, to visit their section. I little thought of spending so much time there when complying with their needs. I found the needs of that field were very great. I began preaching, and proceeded on the theory that there is a spirit in man and that the inspiration of the Almighty giveth him understanding; that men have hearts, and crowds were made conscious of the fact. Hundreds were converted. Houses of worship were filled with hearers. On one occasion, fifty persons, mostly heads of families, were baptized in six days.

But to return to the Southwest. Hearing there was a proselyte at the gate, who had been under the instruction of Bro. Moody for a time, I determined to visit his neighborhood. Bro. Leonard was baptized, and a respectable church was established at Pleasant Hill, Grayson County, embracing several members of the family of Thomas Stone, a Methodist preacher, and a young man of parts and culture. He felt it his duty to defend his Zion, and proposed to discuss Methodism vs. the teachings of the Disciples. I thought it discreet to lift the gauntlet. He attended an appointment I had at Pleasant Hill. At the close of the services he invited me to his house, with the purpose, as I supposed, of arranging for the conflict. On the way, from some remarks he made, I pleasantly suggested the propriety of settling our controversy by his immersion, and was surprised with the serious reply that, with the removal of a few difficulties, he was prepared for such a step. The truth was, he had provided himself with a copy of the Campbell and Rice debate, and there was not much left for discussion. I was very glad to find his difficulties removed, and as the water was not distant, as the sun was setting behind the western hills, he was buried with Christ in baptism. I invited his wife to accompany him in this significant ordinance embracing such a precious promise. Her father, too, was a preacher, and she was unprepared for such a step, but I was glad to see that during a long conversation on the subject before retiring on the night of her husband's baptism, she was a very close and anxious listener. She probably saw that the questions discussed comprehended her difficulties. Certain it is that her husband, very early in the morning, was at my bedside with the intelligence of his wife's desire for baptism. Before my return home they were received into the church, and Bro. Stone was ordained as a minister of the gospel, which he has faithfully proclaimed to this day.

I must notice my first interview with Alexander Campbell. The universal prejudice which existed against him was as blind and unjust with the brethren I had gathered as with the religious denominations. After I had made myself acquainted with his views, and had my own mind disabused of false impressions, knowing what would be the ultimate destiny of the churches I had planted, I hastened to privately inform the minds of brethren that were of reputation, as Paul says, and even to induce them to subscribe for the *Harbinger;* and thus by 1839, when Mr. Campbell was to be in Charlottesville, a public sentiment had been established in the mountains which justified me, with the advice and consent of the churches here, in seeking recognition by the churches in Eastern Virginia. In Charlottesville, I arranged to exchange labors with R.L. Coleman and J.W. Goss, who on visiting us were joyfully received. Their presence relieved the brethren of the fear of what might result to the churches as a consequence of my death. They now felt they were not alone in the world, that there were other defenders of the faith to whom they might look with confidence. Of course I contemplated A. Campbell with the liveliest interest. And, say what we will about human leaders, the cause which had so much of our hearts, was deeply involved in this man. I left Charlottesville greatly encouraged. I had never known a man whom I would place beside A. Campbell. I heard him with delight; and personally he had accepted me for every dime I was worth. I should mention as the other preachers in Eastern Virginia, at the time of this interview with Mr. Campbell, Thomas Henley, James Henshall, Dr. Wm. Pendleton and his nephew, Dr. Madison Pendleton, James Bagby, James W. Goss, Dr. Duval and A.B. Walthall.

I cannot close this brief and partial record of my life without some acknowledgment, of some of its great deficiencies. One prominent wrong was the failure to educate the brethren in the important duty of supplying the sinews of war. The churches in Southwest Virginia and West Virginia, the border counties of North Carolina and Tennessee, and of Southern Piedmont are largely the fruitage of unrequited toil. For twenty-five years I did not receive the equivalent of *my horse's* outfit and expenses. And I am confident that James Miller, of Tennessee, a most excellent preacher, who exchanged labors with me, was scarcely better requited. And how am I to meet G.W. Abell, whom I lured to this field as his home by deducting five hundred dollars from the value of the farm he purchased? I am thankful that he soon saw his mistake in committing himself to churches, which, unspoiled, would have been all his heart could have wished. The truth was, I had discovered the apostolic modes of conversion and sanctification, and it was pay enough to see the grateful tears of the joyful penitent though to me a day of toil and fasting. Thus moved I had no compunction in persuading Cephas Shelburne to settle here, and while toiling for a growing family, at the same time supplying with no little labor and travel weekly, sermons of no ordinary merit for twenty years without a shadow of compensation. And yet Brother Walthall lies heavier on my conscience, who came to supply my place while battling with materialism in Southeast Virginia. Last night memory confronted me with his cold, but patient face, as he was urging his horse "Charlie," to one of his appointments. I claim credit for not distinguishing between my kin and others. D.A. Snow was the principal agent in building the Wytheville Church, and, I may add, that my business connection with his father enabled me to do more preaching than I otherwise would have done.

In controversies which could not be avoided, I was not always lamb-like. The truth is, I was rendered almost desperate by the proscriptions in every form save in assaults upon my character. I certainly lacked gentleness. Crossing swords with a Presbyterian preacher I did not properly respect his ripe years, sound scholarship and highly valued labors. With a milder manner the venerable Geo. Fainter's feelings would have been spared. If we could only learn an easier way than by experience. But this is a road we never travel but once, and our mistakes have to survive us.

To my loving brethren and my still more loving heavenly Father, with a grateful remembrance of all the kindness of earth and heaven, I close, with all the forbearance I can speak, this short sketch of what I have attempted in the name of my Lord and

Master. I referred to the failure of my parents to impress my young mind with God's goodness. It has just occurred to me that the fear with which I regarded him was, to a great extent, caused by the pall that hung over my family for thirteen years from the harrowing anxieties for the fate of a brother stolen when four years old. I am certain I never saw father or mother, or either of my two sisters laugh until he was recovered when I was nine years of age. Such a grief-stricken family was not calculated to inspire a sense of a loving God. Jacob's believing that Joseph had been torn by wild beasts cannot compare with the grief of parents knowing their children were in the hands of sinful captors.

Part Three:
Frederick Power Remembers Chester Bullard

It is to be regretted that this good man has left us no account of his later service. While these imperfect notes furnish some idea of his early struggles to plant the cause of primitive Christianity in Southwest Virginia, for many years after Dr. Bullard joined his forces with these of the greater leader he did a splendid work and preached the gospel far and wide, organizing churches and baptizing thousands. No history of the reformatory work of Mr. Campbell and his co-laborers can be perfect without taking into account the movement in the Virginia mountains, of which this man was the inspiration. He was incessant and unwearied in his labors as an evangelist, traveling on horseback through the mountains and enduring great hardships. Three thousand souls were gathered into the fold in Southwest Virginia through his efforts, and perhaps seventy-five churches established, either directly or indirectly, through his influence, in that section alone. His preaching tours extended frequently to other parts of the State, and wherever he went large crowds attended his meetings, and hundreds and even thousands obeyed the gospel.

The writer first met him in Eastern Virginia in 1867 and 1868. He was then well advanced in life, but still a vigorous and laborious preacher. He stood about five feet eight inches, and weighed perhaps a hundred and fifty pounds. He had a patriarchal appearance, wearing a long grey beard, and beneath shaggy eyebrows sparkled small dark grey eyes that had a wonderful glow during his powerful exhortations. He was not strictly a logical reasoner in his sermons, but he was very impassioned often, and always commanded the closest attention. He dealt chiefly with "First Principles," Christ the foundation, the conversions in the New Testament, the union of Christians on the Bible alone, the gospel, the power of God unto salvation. His sermons, while sufficiently clear in statement of doctrine, were largely given to declamation and exhortation. He had a magnificent voice, which evidently had been much abused by the constant tax of outdoor preaching and unceasing exercise in the pulpit and out of it, but was still impressive and powerful. In exhortation he was specially gifted, and would plead with the people with great tenderness and untiring perseverance, urging them in repeated appeals so long as one would come to confess Christ. And this apostolic labor was not only in the public meetings but from house to house. He would go among all classes and talk to them in their homes of the love of Christ for human souls. D.A. Snow traveled with him as early as 1838, when he was seventeen years of age, leading the singing and aiding him in prayer and exhortation, and he tells many interesting experiences connected with the doctor's labors among the mountains, visiting the very poor, sleeping in log cabins, and sharing with the humblest people in their frugal bounty. The converts were then known as "Bullardites," and an ex-Methodist brother by the name of Shepherd was well known throughout that region for his daily prayer at his home altar for his "brudder Methodists that they might all be converted and come over and jine Bullard!"

Dr. Bullard was noted for his kindness to young people, and especially his encouragement to young men to preach the gospel. The writer would, in this public manner, acknowledge his own obligations to this noble servant of Jesus Christ. He organized in the churches, where he held meetings, young men's prayer-meetings for the training of young converts. He would himself write out a constitution and meet with the young men and boys and talk to them, teach them how to pray, call on them to follow him in prayer, and help them in their feeble attempts to utter their petitions. Such a prayer-meeting he organized in a schoolhouse at the home of my father, which was continued for years by the handful of boys which constituted it, though most of them lived miles away from the place of meeting, and out of that little gathering, which had an average attendance of seven, with no other exercises than Bible reading, prayer and song, came three preachers of the gospel. The good fruits of this faithful man's excessive labors in the gospel, are to be found everywhere in Virginia, and out of it in many places.

Doctor Bullard was married four times. His first wife was Eley K. Pierce, of Montgomery County; his second, Adeline Stone, of Lunenburg County; his third, Mary Dunkum, of Albemarle, the mother of William S. Bullard, and his last wife was Elizabeth Craig, of Pulaski County. He had only three children, and but one survives him, his son W.S. Bullard, a bright and pure man, and a faithful preacher of the cross, who inherits much of his father's eloquence and enthusiasm without, we regret to say, his physical powers of endurance. Few men have been more richly endowed in mind and body for such a pioneer service than Dr. Bullard. He blazed the way for others, and endured hardness as a true soldier of Jesus Christ. He had the lion-like qualities of courage and persistence and a right of command. His trust in God was very beautiful, and his spirit of piety was felt by all who came in contact with him, but by nature he had a strong element of conscious personality and leadership. He was a man whose affections were warm and deep. His sermons were full of an unction that stirred souls to their depths. His appeals were often overpowering in their earnestness and heartfulness. He won the children to him, and he was always welcome in the homes of the people, leaving behind him, wherever he came, a benediction. For threescore years he proclaimed the gospel story, and told it with a simplicity and a power that was irresistible, as thousands dead and alive would joyfully bear witness. It was a positive exhilaration to him to preach. His industry was indefatigable, his courage undaunted, his zeal for souls a consuming fire. God acknowledged the work of his servant and blessed him abundantly. Gradually his labors were lessened, and sustained by his unfaltering trust in his Master and the loving ministries of his family and friends he came to the close of his earthly pilgrimage. He entered calmly upon his rest, and on the first day of March, eleven days before the completion of his eighty-fourth year, the worn body was put away in its last resting place on the hillside over-looking his old home, "Humility," near the village of Snowville, there to await the resurrection when this vile body shall be fashioned like unto the glorious body of the Son of God. For him to live was Christ, and to die was gain.

I am glad in closing this brief tribute to so faithful a life to be able to lay before my readers a synopsis of Dr. Bullard's famous sermon on "Christian Union"—one which he was often called upon to repeat over and over again at the same place, and sometimes during the same meeting.

Part Four:
Sermon on Christian Union

John 17:21-22: "That Christianity will ultimately triumph is assured by prophecy and promises, but never by a mutinous church, ignoring both the plan and the spirit of its author, can this be done. Union is an indispensable condition through all the vegetable, animal, and spiritual realms of the universe, as illustrated in our Lord's parable of the vine and its branches. When the little worm under the bark has encircled the mighty oak its doom is fixed. When the late planted is overtaken by the early frost, splitting every conduit of life, the lifeless blades soon shiver over the blasted hopes of the laggard husbandman. On the battlefield we see in every instrument of death an instrument of schism, intended to mutilate God's image. And I believe, like the worm under the bark, every disease intercepting the vital fluid is only the power wielded by the rider of the pale horse. Spiritually we know what the result is of a separation from him who is the life of the world. Just as the branch dies, deprived of the sap, so a member of Christ's body, drawn away and enticed by dogma, dies spiritually, becomes no longer life inspiring, but only poisons the stream of life for those with whom he is connected.

"Our great Lord and Master has staked all the benefits of his mission to inspire a principle, which can be spelled with four letters, in the hearts of his retainers. This principle can only be possessed and wielded by the pure in heart—only by those begotten of God. There is not a sectarian in the whole band. Many Christians have been captured, but not one of them sectarian in heart, and when one of God's children is brought in contact with a kindred spirit, they will unite as drops of water. Though one of them may have encumbered himself with a thousand notions or doctrines, it no more quenches the flame of his unencumbered brother's love than the dirt on the face of the little child quenches its mother's sympathies. And this love must either secure the world's conversion and union, or the mission of Christ is a failure.

"The parentage of sectarianism is given by the apostle James when he tells of the origin of wars and fightings. Paul asks of those infected with this spirit 'Are you not carnal, and walk as men?' And again: 'If ye bite and devour one another, take heed that ye be not consumed one of another.' Do you say not all that are incorporated in sectarian ranks bite and devour one another? Then they are in the wrong pew, for all true sectarians have terrible teeth. Read the account of the birth of any religious party. The church has assembled to deliver over to Satan a brother guilty of a thought not colored like their own and he is cast out, though he would give his life to share the love of those who love his Master. This is sectarianism. It is simply the absence of love, which seeks union with every kindred spirit. It now exists in Church and State. Its whole soul is selfishness. A young angel, in care of an old one bearing dispatches to this earth, descended upon the scene of the battle of Trafalgar and accused his escort of having brought him to hell. They say a sectarian was once found in heaven. Why not leave him there, since it is said sects are good things on earth. You would not send him to hell since its tenants do not deserve good things. I think our first parents would have done better without him. If you doubt the existence of Christians under Sectarian banners, bring two who love their Saviour together, out of sight of their leaders; let them converse about the kingdom of God and his righteousness, and behold the loving tears and heaving bosoms and the joyful anticipation of meeting where there will be no more separation, and the ardent wish that they might have a blessed time here as well. Is the question asked, how are they kept apart here? It has been done by authoritatively requiring unanimity of sentiment as a basis of Christian fellowship, thus virtually discarding Christ as the basis of the Church, of whom Paul says: 'Other foundation can no man lay then is laid, which is Jesus Christ.' When the Eunuch said: 'Here is water, what doth hinder me from being baptized?' Philip answered: 'If thou believest with all thine heart thou mayest.' And he was at once baptized, not into any sect or party, but into Christ, or, as Paul says, 'built upon the one foundation.'

"As love is indispensable to Christian character, and as nobody can love a creed, or, indeed, anything in all the universe but a person, so Satan never told a bigger falsehood, or a more mischievous one, than when he suggested building a Christian church on any other foundation than on a living, loving Christ, who could inspire love in these united to him. Now, if we know what Philip preached, and by what action he baptized the Eunuch, we would know how to build a church against which the gates of hell would not prevail; and they never did prevail until the primitive church began to formulate creeds, such as 'Except ye be circumcised, and keep the law of Moses, ye can not be saved'; and

'I am of Paul' and 'I am of Apollos,' thus virtually ignoring the foundation laid in Zion.

"Some apologists for division will say: 'Union is impossible, because all cannot think alike.' Do all Christians think as God thinks, or a child of twelve as a sage of fifty? Who, by requiring it, would lord it ever God's heritage? How long does anyone retain the thoughts of today? In only one thing are we required to think alike—that Jesus Christ is truly the Son of God, that he loved us better than his life, and that to obey him is the whole duty of man. Now this is what every Christian thinks. No two Christians have different Lords, faiths or Spirits; and as soon as they love God as they should and as the necessities of a perishing world require, they will find one baptism and not have to blush in the presence of a pagan whom they have crossed the ocean to serve.

"After all the efforts Christians have made to believe what they think is inevitable that sects and parties are good things of the Holy Spirit in them gives it the lie and is grieved at their efforts to prove it true. Just as well believe that it is not good for the members of a family to dwell together in unity; that brothers, sisters, husbands and wives should war with each other. If the members of Christ's body should wake some morning with the intelligence that the representatives of the different churches had agreed to unite on a single article—faith in the living Christ—ignoring as a condition of union every debatable question that has hitherto divided the church, what a shout of joy would go up to heaven rolling under its broad archway. There is no event in the annals of time that has so thrilled the human heart as this would move it. When the world was created the morning stars sang together and all the sons of God shouted for joy, but that event was not to be compared with the world teeming with inhabitants being conquered for Christ. When Jesus was born in Bethlehem the shepherds did well to worship the babe in the manger, the wise men to present their gifts of gold, frankincense and myrrh, Simeon and Anna to take the young child in their arms and bless him, the angels to sing their choral, 'Glory to God in the highest peace on earth, good will to men; but none of them knew the import of his birth. The prophets searched diligently how and what manner of time the spirit that was in them did signify when it spake beforehand of the sufferings of Christ and the glory that should follow. The glory was to succeed the union of his blood-bought followers.

"I have already said that we can only love persons. I now say we only deeply love those who so love us as to be willing to suffer for us. Our children only love us because we first loved them; and every family will be found a quarreling family unrestrained by devoted parental love. We love Christ because he first loved us. He said: 'If I be lifted up I will draw all men unto me'; and the apostle said, `I determined not to know anything among you but Christ and him crucified.' Here we have Christ's whole philosophy of Christian union, and by uniting his prayer with his life we have it illustrated. It was a Jew that approached the Samaritan woman, and the man who has not realized the animus of the two days domiciled in Shechem will probably go into the next world only partially acquainted with his Master. See him apparently throwing himself away in calling Zaccheus from the sycamore tree, and you will see in the gratitude of his host that he was searching for hearts which in this case and in Matthew's he could distinguish underneath their callings. Not less is this evident in the sinful woman who anointed his feet in the house of Simon. And see him selecting a Samaritan in his prince of parables, and almost with his last breath pouring salvation on the wretch that languished at his side."

It is no wonder, when this devoted preacher of the cross pleaded during the sixty years of his unselfish ministry in such loving terms for the oneness of God's people, that thousands discarded their human standards, and accepted the divine basis. The times call for just such earnest, honest, tender and apostolic service now. Let this heroic example move our young men; let such great characters abide with us; let bind ourselves by all that is sacred, that the fruits of such noble toil and sacrifice shall not perish from the earth.

About The Author

Frederick D. Power is a Virginian. He was born January 23, 1851, within a few miles of historic Yorktown, and was the second of nine children. His father, Dr. Robert Henry Power, was a well-known physician, and served in both houses of the State Legislature. His grandfather, Dr. Frederick Bryan Power, was a Baptist, and old Grafton church, where the family worshiped, was founded in 1813. The congregation accepted Alexander Campbell's position and he visited them in 1856.

Mr. Power's mother was Abigail M. Jencks, of DeRuyter, Madison County, N.Y. She was educated at Mrs. Willard's famous Troy Female Seminary; was a teacher and a woman of exceptional culture and beautiful character. He received his early education from his mother. When he was a boy of ten years of age, the Civil War broke out and his home was in the track of the armies. Big Bethel, the first battle, was fought within three miles, and the battle between the Merrimac and Monitor, the siege of Yorktown, and battle of Williamsburg were nearby. During these four years there were no schools. Then for three years his father employed a teacher in the home, but two winters he was in Richmond as a page in the State Senate. He obeyed the gospel under the preaching of A.B. Walthall, when fifteen years of age, and in September, 1868, entered Bethany College to prepare for the ministry. Three years were spent in Bethany. During the vacations he preached in Eastern Virginia, and for several months, in 1870, served the church at Washington, Pa., while a student. Graduating in 1871, he was ordained at Mathew's C.H. at the Tidewater Convention, August 13, by Robert Y. Henley, Peter Ainslie, and J. W. Williams, and took charge of Smyrna church, King and Queen County, Jerusalem, King William, and Olive Branch, James City County. These congregations were far apart, means of transportation difficult, and his labors were severe, but he regarded the two years spent with these country churches as of inestimable value to him. The second year, instead of Jerusalem, he served his old home church, Grafton.

January, 1874, Mr. Power accepted the church in Charlottesville, Va., the seat of the University, with the purpose of taking lectures at that institution. One Lord's Day was given to Gilboa, Louisa County. March 17th of that year, he married Miss Emily Browne Alsop, of Fredericksburg, and in September was called to Bethany College as adjunct professor of ancient languages. His salary as pastor was $500 a year. The year spent at Bethany was one of great profit to him, being associated with his old professors, Pendleton and Loos. He preached during the session at West Liberty, W. Va. In May, 1875, he was called to Washington, D. C., and declined the invitation. Afterward, by a personal visit of one of the elders of the church, he was induced to visit them, and the result was an engagement upon which he entered in September.

For twenty-eight years he has been pastor of the Vermont avenue church. He found a little frame chapel, with 150 members, poor and little known in the city. It was a hard struggle. In 1880, General Garfield was elected to the Presidency and great interest centered about "the little Campbellite shanty" and its little flock. A new church building was erected and dedicated in 1884, and the church has now a property worth $70,000. In 1881, Mr. Power was made Chaplain of the House of Representatives, to which office he was chosen by acclamation.

Three other churches have been formed from the Vermont Avenue church, the Ninth Street, H Street, and Whitney Avenue; and three others are about to be added to them: The Fifth church, in the Southeastern part of the city, Antioch, near Vienna, Va. and Woodridge. The mother church has a membership of 625. Through the influence of this church the Christian Missionary Society of Maryland, Delaware, and District of Columbia, was organized October, 1878, of which Mr. Power was president for twenty years.

The subject of this sketch is six feet in height and weighs 195 pounds. Since he was thirty years of age his hair has been grey, and he is often taken for a venerable man. He received from Bethany the honorary degrees of A.M. and LL.D., and has been for years a trustee of that institution. He is also a trustee of the United Society of Christian Endeavor. He was for many years a correspondent of the *Christian Standard,* and is at present associate editor of the *Christian Evangelist.* He is the author of a Life of W. K. Pendleton, Bible Doctrine for Young People, Sketches of Our

Pioneers, etc. He is also a lecturer, and frequently appears on Chautauqua platforms and in lecture courses. His life has been a very busy and a very happy one.